The Friendship Book

A THOUGHT FOR EACH DAY IN 2012

"The greatest sweetener of human life is friendship."

Joseph Addison

January

Sunday – ***January 1***

SUNDAY MORNING WALK

EARLY,
As birds rose,
I stepped into a sun-shaped glen
Filled with a congregation of ferns
Bent in worship,
Hushed in contemplation –
A small, sacred secret
Kept by a silent forest.
For an eternity
I stood
And then, summoned,
Knelt quietly
Among their fragrant praise.

Rachel Wallace-Oberle

Monday – ***January 2***

HAVE you made any New Year Resolutions? How many? Not so many, I hope, that there's no room for me to suggest one more.

I borrowed it from the eighteenth-century English clergyman Sydney Smith. He was the very wise man who wrote: "When you rise in the morning make a resolution to make the day a happy one for a fellow creature."

Now, there's a resolution that's worth keeping all year round!

Tuesday — ***January 3***

MANY of us probably look to a new year with a mixture of emotions. Sadness at things gone by, perhaps, concern for what may lie ahead, but many of us still look ahead to a new year with an almost childish sense of excitement for all the, as yet, undiscovered possibilities the future holds during the next 12 months.

Joni Eareckson Tada describes that same feeling when she says: "God specialises in things fresh and firsthand. His plans for you this year may outshine those of the past."

So, here's to the new year ahead of us all and all things fresh!

Wednesday — ***January 4***

"IT'S my collections that I'll miss the most," Audrey had lamented when she prepared to move from her large, rambling house to a small bungalow. "I'm looking forward to moving, but there simply won't be space for all my tea-sets, my postcards and my china pigs. I'll have to think of something different that takes up less room."

So the Lady of the House was intrigued when she went to visit Audrey's new home. She was immediately invited indoors to see a new collection.

"Here it is," Audrey smiled mischievously, flourishing a small notebook.

"You see, I'm collecting happy moments," she explained. "Whenever something really nice happens, I write it down. The only trouble is, I'm already running out of space. This is my second notebook!"

No home is too small for that kind of collection.

Seeking The Sunlight

Thursday — **January 5**

ONE day, our old friend Mary was talking about what she called "the Gift of Joy". It made me think, because joy is a wonderful gift, isn't it? It doesn't have anything to do with great occasions, celebrations or achievements.

Joy is something we feel deep inside us. It can happen suddenly and unexpectedly and when we feel it, we should cherish it and share our elation with others.

Mother Teresa was able to find it in the harshest conditions. "A joyful heart is the inevitable result of a heart burning with love," she said.

I hope we can all feel that way and share our precious gift.

Friday — **January 6**

IF everyone swept in front of their own house, the whole town would be clean, advises an old Polish proverb. These days it could well refer to the kind of community effort that makes environmental projects like recycling, efficient energy use and litter collection really work.

If we take to heart a modern interpretation of these words, we could all work together to make the world a better place. Something to think about today.

Saturday — **January 7**

OUR young friend Daniel caught sight of these words posted on his school's notice board: *Personality may open doors, but character keeps them open.*

Well said, indeed!

Sunday – ***January 8***

THE lessons from the story of Noah and the Ark are surely to plan ahead, remember that it wasn't raining when the journey began, build a future on solid ground, and have a good friend so you can travel in pairs. Not least, don't worry if you are not in the fast lane – the snails climbed aboard safely, too.

Remember, too, that whenever you are feeling preoccupied, it is good to relax and float awhile. A flood of good advice, don't you agree?

"But with thee I will establish my covenant; and thou shalt come into the Ark, then, and thy sons, and thy wife, and thy sons' wives with thee." (Genesis 6-18)

Monday – ***January 9***

ONE of the most striking moments in the life of the Scottish mountaineer, William Hutchinson Murray, occurred not on the mountains but in the desert near El Alamein.

Murray was captured in the middle of the night by a German tank commander who jokingly asked if he wasn't feeling the cold. "It's as cold as a mountain top," Murray replied. The German officer asked, "You climb mountains?"

"He was a mountaineer," Murray recalled. "We both relaxed. He stuffed his gun away. After a few quick words – the Alps, Scotland, rock and ice – he could not do enough for me."

It's a fine reminder that on a global scale, war, politics and nationality might come between us, but on a one-to-one level our loves, passions and interests are often the same the whole world over.

It's the things we have in common that bring us together.

Tuesday – ***January 10***

"OH, dear," June said, "I did make a mix-up of it all." She was explaining to the Lady of the House how she'd forgotten a friend's birthday, had tried to make amends with a bunch of flowers, only to remember too late that her friend was allergic to pollen. Happily the episode had ended in chuckles, but June was still regretting her choice of gift.

All the same, the tale did remind me of some words from Lucy Maud Montgomery, whose Anne of Green Gables was more accident-prone than most: "Isn't it nice to think that tomorrow is a new day with no mistakes in it yet?"

Now that's a thought to make anyone feel better!

Wednesday – ***January 11***

KENNY, a friend who is a keen sailor, keeps this framed saying below decks and I'd say it applies to sailors and landlubbers alike:

Both faith and fear might sail into your harbour, but it's your harbour and you decide who gets to drop anchor.

Thursday – ***January 12***

IT'S one of those phrases we all seem to have said – or had said to us by a frustrated parent: "If all your friends were to jump off a bridge, would you jump with them?"

Well, one day I heard that idea turned around and used as a beautiful description of friendship. "If all his friends were to jump off a bridge," the speaker said, "he wouldn't jump with them. He'd already be there at the bottom, waiting to catch them!"

Snow And
Silhouette

Friday – **January 13**

ROGER is one of the directors of an international charity organisation and is committed to its aim to support those in danger of starvation. When asked how he remains inspired, he referred to a beautiful quote by the author, artist and theologian, Kent Nerburn.

"Remember to be gentle with yourself and others. We are all children of chance and none can say why some fields will blossom while others lay brown beneath the August sun. Care for those around you. Look past your differences. Their dreams are no less than yours, their choices no more easily made.

"And give, give in any way you can, of whatever you possess. To give is to love. To withhold is to wither. Care less for your harvest than for how it is shared and your life will have meaning and your heart will have peace."

Saturday – **January 14**

EVERY journey changes us,
No matter near or far,
Each step into uncharted lands,
Can alter who we are.
For as we travel so we start
To see our world anew,
We talk with strangers on our way,
We see a different view.
And so we learn to tolerate,
To understand, to grow,
For every journey changes us
Wherever we may go.

Margaret Ingall.

Sunday – ***January 15***

THE great composer Johann Sebastian Bach began his manuscripts with the initials JJ and he ended them with the initials SDG. JJ, it turns out, stood for *Jesu Juva*, or *Jesus Help Me*. SDG meant *Soli Dei Gratia*, or *To God Alone Go The Thanks*.

Between the request for inspiration and the gratitude for help received lay some of the most beautiful music ever written:

"For everyone who asks receives; he who seeks finds; and to him who knocks the door shall be opened."
(Matthew 7.8)

Monday – ***January 16***

THERE'S an Asian legend which told of a man who wanted to give up. Nothing was going his way at all, it seemed, so he went into the forest to explain to God why he'd had enough.

God listened, then told the man about the time, before the forest, when he had planted the first fern and bamboo seeds. After a year, the fern sprouted, but there was no sign of the bamboo. He didn't give up.

After another year the fern had spread, but the bamboo couldn't be seen. He still didn't give up. In the third and fourth years the ferns covered swathes of ground. The bamboo still hadn't made an appearance. However, even then God didn't give up.

In the fifth year the bamboo broke the surface – and grew a total of one hundred feet in six months! During the lean years the bamboo had worked hard, putting down strong roots, so when its time came to grow, nothing would stop it.

I hope the man who wanted to give up had a change of heart.

Tuesday — ***January 17***

HOW do you fancy doing a "paper-burst"? You know, it's similar to when a hidden celebrity suddenly jumps through a brightly-coloured paper screen to the delight of an audience.

A man by the name of Brendan Francis suggested a way each of us can have that experience – and become stronger in the process. "Many of our fears are tissue paper thin," he wrote, "and a single courageous step would carry us clear through them."

Wednesday — ***January 18***

WINTER nights have a magic of their own – if you can savour one when it isn't raining or blowing a storm! I like to stand under a clear winter's sky and look up at the stars. There are more than you could ever count and more than you ever catch sight of in summer time.

But it seems there's an old Inuit or Eskimo tradition that stars aren't stars – rather they are seen as holes in the sky where the love of our departed ones shines through to show us how happy they are.

A beautiful idea to think about today.

Thursday — ***January 19***

MARIA sent the Lady of the House a postcard while holidaying in New Zealand. She was intrigued to share this proverb Maria had heard on her travels: *Turn your face to the sun and the shadows fall behind you.*

Words worth considering, don't you agree?

Friday – ***January 20***

THREE hundred years ago in Japan, the Great Tea Master Soshitsu Sen asked the question, "What is the most wonderful thing for people like me who follow the Way of Tea?"

The answer was, "The oneness felt by host and guest when they meet heart to heart and share a bowl of tea."

Is it any wonder that the tradition of a nice cup of tea is still going strong?

Saturday – ***January 21***

HERE'S an intriguing Spanish proverb I came across while reading a book of daily reflections: *A wise man changes his mind, a fool never.*

Good advice to keep in mind at all times, don't you agree?

Sunday – ***January 22***

HAVE you heard of Laminin? Neither had I, until a biologist friend explained. Laminin is the substance that sticks one living cell to another – it is quite literally the stuff that stops us from falling apart.

Then he showed me a molecular diagram of Laminin. It's a long, vertical line with a shorter, horizontal line crossing it about a third of the way down.

In other words, at the most basic level you can get, it's a cross that holds every one of us together!

"He is before all things, and in him all things hold together."
(Colossians 1:17)

Monday – ***January 23***

MANY of us go to bed at night with the cares of the day still on our mind. The sixteenth-century nobleman Sir William Cecil seemed to have the answer to the problem.

During a spell in charge of the nation's Treasury he was reputed to throw his ceremonial robe on the bedroom floor each evening, saying, "Lie there, Lord Treasurer." Then he would sleep soundly as an ordinary man, undisturbed by affairs of State.

It's a tip worth taking for a good night's sleep. I just wonder if throwing my socks on the floor would have the same effect.

Tuesday – ***January 24***

IS life often incredibly busy for you with very few moments to spare? If so, here is a thought from our old friend Anon:

"One of the greatest labour-saving inventions of all time is – tomorrow!"

Wednesday – ***January 25***

THE Lady of the House found this little poem by an unknown author in a well-thumbed book of charming verses and I'd like to share it with you today:

When the wind blows,
that is my medicine.
When it rains,
that is my medicine.
When it hails,
that is my medicine.
When it becomes clear after a storm,
that is my medicine.

Thursday — ***January 26***

IN 1869 entrepreneur Henry John Heinz founded Heinz, a company that now sells many millions of bottles of its much-loved ketchup every year and provides food to families in 200 countries around the world.

Mr Heinz said: "To do a common thing uncommonly well brings success."

How very true!

Friday — ***January 27***

I'D known Anna for several years before I realised what she was doing. It occurred to me that this popular woman rarely said "no" or "but" in conversation. Instead she made good use of the phrase, "Yes, and …" That way she stays positive, moves the discussion forward and invites the other person to keep contributing to whatever the subject is.

"Isn't that a bit sneaky?" I asked.

"Yes," Anna replied with a smile. "And?"

My reply was almost involuntarily positive. "And . . . it works!"

Saturday — ***January 28***

THE Roman playwright Plautus is perhaps best remembered for his comedies. He even adopted the name Maccius after a traditional clown figure. But he could be serious about some things and was especially serious about the value of friendship.

"Nothing but heaven itself," he wrote, "is better than a friend who is really a friend."

Sunday – ***January 29***

I WAS reading about the wonders of modern technology and this brought to mind something I was reading about Alan Tennant and his attempts to track peregrine falcons on their migration routes.

Despite radio tags, satellite links and an aeroplane to follow them in, he regularly lost track of these endangered birds and had to search them out again. How much more impressive would be a power that could track every falcon in the world all the time – along with every other creature, on land, in the sea or on the wing?

"Are not five sparrows sold for two pennies? Yet not one of them is forgotten by God." (Luke 12:6)

Monday – ***January 30***

I RECENTLY read some words by an unknown wit which said, "Being young is beautiful, but being old is comfortable."

I prefer to think of it as, "Being young is beautiful but very hard work! And being old is when you get to put your feet up and reap the rewards of all that work."

Tuesday – ***January 31***

I WONDER if you know these memorable lines written by Ralph Waldo Emerson:

"We take care of our health; we lay up money; we make our roof tight, and our clothing sufficient; but who provides wisely that he shall not be wanting in the best property of all – friends?"

Thoughtful words to keep in mind – always.

Smooth As Silk

February

Wednesday – **February 1**

THE well-loved writer of children's stories, Charles Kingsley, was getting on in years when a Mrs Browning asked him, "What is the secret of your life? Tell me, that I might make mine beautiful too."

Mr Kingsley replied, "I had a friend."

A "secret" that would make any life beautiful!

Thursday –**February 2**

THOMAS' secondary school class decided to join the Make Poverty History campaign by going on a "24-hour famine". They refrained from eating their usual meals and camped out at school in their sleeping bags; into the early hours of the morning they played games, sang and discussed social issues, such as better worldwide aid, with their teacher.

Thomas and his friends were so encouraged by the substantial sum of sponsorship money raised that they decided to join others in sending a message to the Minister for International Cooperation in support of legislation to help end global poverty. These compassionate, concerned teenagers are part of a call to action that now runs campaigns in more than 80 countries.

When many voices speak at once, their message cannot be ignored.

Friday — **February 3**

I KNOW it's a bit of a cliché to speak of life being like a journey, but I couldn't help smiling when Lucy started to elaborate on the idea:

"Sometimes," she told the Lady of the House, "I feel as if I'm racing through the day as smoothly as a gazelle. Sometimes it's as if I'm a tiny gastropod, just creeping along at a snail's pace. And sometimes," she added, ruefully, "I just have to be like a frog and take a great big leap of faith!"

Well, that's the way to make a splash in the world!

Saturday — **February 4**

RECENTLY our old friend Mary had a series of mishaps of a non-serious, but highly irritating nature. In the midst of her exasperation, a friend sent her a card that contained this message: *The only way to see a rainbow is to look through the rain.*

Ideal to keep in mind whenever heavy showers start to fall on our patch!

Sunday — **February 5**

HAVE you ever visited the delightful little village of Clovelly on the North Devon coast? A reader sent me a copy of The Clovelly Fishermen's Prayer and I'd like to share it with you today:

Almighty and all merciful Father, who rulest heaven and earth and sea and all deep places; at whose word the storm wind ariseth, and again at Thy word the great calm; Receive into Thy protection Thy servants the fishermen, in their honest calling; that through calm or storm they may come in with safety; for the sake of Him who rules the waves, Jesus Christ our Lord. Amen.

Monday — **February 6**

THE weeks are moving forward,
As every year they must,
And many resolutions lie
Forgotten in the dust.
But as we seek the road ahead,
Lord, show us You are near,
To light the way and smooth the path
And wipe away each tear.

The snowdrops peeping through the earth
Remind us life goes on,
And we can find new hope and strength
When doubt and fear are gone.
Now as we watch the seasons change,
Lord, teach us how to live,
And how to share the joy of life
And all the gifts You give.

Iris Hesselden

Tuesday — **February 7**

DESPITE not having a written language by the time the European settlers arrived in North America, the native peoples there had languages that were as intricate as any from elsewhere. Often, in fact, their language was much more colourful and descriptive.

I was especially inspired by the definition of the word "friend" which, to many of the tribes was, "the one who carries my sorrows on his back". Wouldn't it be wonderful to have a friend like that, and wouldn't it be even better if we could be a friend like that?

Scottish Splendour

Wednesday – **February 8**

I ONCE read about a girl who started keeping a list of things that made her smile. Twenty years later she published her collection under the name, "14,000 Things To Be Happy About".

Now, I'm not a mathematician but 14,000 things over 20 years ... Well, that's about two a day. Every day, you may ask?

Well, here's another day. Let's look out for these things to be happy about!

Thursday – **February 9**

CONTEMPLATE this Buddhist prayer of peace and reflect on its meaning today:

May I become at all times, both now and forever
A protector for those without protection,
A guide for those who have lost their way
A ship for those with oceans to cross,
A bridge for those with rivers to cross
A sanctuary for those in danger,
A lamp for those without light
A place of refuge for those who lack shelter –
And a servant to all in need.

Friday – **February 10**

ANTHONY'S garden is his haven. Endless hours are spent tending his flowers and enjoying their beauty and over the years, he has lovingly created an entrance with stepping stones and a trellis. It bears a plaque that says: *Keep your eyes to the skies, your feet on the path and your heart in the moment.*

What a lovely way to walk through life's garden!

Saturday – ***February 11***

WE would all like to know how to live our lives well, and grow old both gracefully and with grace. Perhaps that much-loved Scottish writer Robert Louis Stevenson points the way about how to do that when he wrote these thought-provoking words:

"To love playthings well as a child, to lead an adventurous and honourable youth, and to settle, when the time arrives, into a green and smiling age, is to be a good artist in life and deserve well of yourself and your neighbour."

Surely there is a wise philosophy of life to be found in these words?

Sunday – ***February 12***

THERE are many attractions to be found on Guernsey, but one of the most inspiring is, for me, the Little Chapel. Built and rebuilt by Brother Déodat during his lifetime, the exterior looks like a magnificent cathedral, but the interior measures a mere nine feet by six feet.

What really makes the Little Chapel stand out, though, is the decor. The whole building glitters in the sunlight, because it is studded with broken crockery and glass!

Now, if Brother Déodat could make something so beautiful from objects that were broken, what might God make of us with our flaws and imperfections? Something to think about today.

"And the God of all grace, who called you to his eternal glory in Christ, after you have suffered a little while, will himself restore you and make you strong, firm and steadfast."

(Peter 1 5:10)

Festival Finery

Monday – **February 13**

ROSEMARY, a proud dog owner, laughed. She'd just told the Lady of the House what age her Golden Labrador was and seen that familiar look of surprise.

"Everyone thinks he's older," she said. "We had an old dog in the house when he arrived as a pup. He copied everything the older pet did. Soon he even had that 'old dog' walk!"

It takes a lot of moral courage not to adopt the habits of the people around us. The "old before its time" dog reminds us that we will eventually walk like the people we walk with.

So surround yourself with people whose habits you wouldn't mind sharing, and share some good habits of your own with them. Then you can walk tall, no matter what height or age you are!

Tuesday – **February 14**

IT wasn't until she came across an old scrapbook that Greta Winton learned more about a piece of her husband's past previously unknown to her. In the late 1930s, as a young London banker, he had single-handedly organised the rescue of hundreds of Jewish refugee children who were stranded in Czechoslovakia after their parents had been seized by the Nazis.

It was a friend who alerted Nicholas Winton to their plight, but it was he who set up base in Prague, working late into the night to raise money, searching for foster parents in Britain and arranging for the children's evacuation by air, rail and sea.

"Don't be content in your life just to do no wrong. Be prepared every day to try to do some good," Nicholas Winton said. It was that philosophy to which many owe their lives today.

Wednesday – ***February 15***

ONE day new lights were installed on our street and many of the beautiful old trees that overhung the pavement were trimmed back. One tree had to be cut back so extensively that the Lady of the House was concerned for its survival.

When she asked an expert to come and look at the tree, she was told the cuts were perfectly acceptable and had been made in the correct places, and because of this the condition of the tree would actually improve.

That incident reminded me a little of life. Sometimes an uncomfortable adjustment is exactly what's required to produce better results!

Thursday – ***February 16***

I READ about a football coach who allowed his team "The 24-Hour Rule". They had that number of hours to celebrate victory or mope about a defeat. Then it was back to normal!

It reminded me of Rudyard Kipling's comment about triumph and disaster: "Those two imposters," he called them.

Life, regardless of its ups and downs, its victories or defeats, its triumphs or disasters, is still a privilege and a treat and the sooner we learn to see it like that, the more we enjoy it. And that's a lifetime rule!

Friday – ***February 17***

THE ancient Chinese were indeed perceptive when they coined the proverb, "Deal with the faults of others as gently as you would your own."

Saturday – ***February 18***

IN life there are many challenges. Some we take on and complete, others might look too big so we leave them aside for another day, but of course "another day" rarely comes. Maybe the difficulty lies not in the challenge, but in how we tackle it.

Nottinghamshire-born writer Samuel Butler left us these words, as relevant today as they were in the nineteenth century when he wrote them:

"If we attend continually and promptly to the little that we can do, we shall ere long be surprised to find how little remains that we cannot do."

Sunday – ***February 19***

THERE are many legends associated with Alexander the Great – but this one hints at a greater truth. One of Alexander's courtiers was having money problems so he asked for a loan. He was told to ask the treasurer for as much as he wanted. So he asked for a huge amount!

When he heard the sum requested Alexander laughed. "In asking for so much," he said, "he has honoured both the wealth of my treasury and the depth of my generosity." The cheeky courtier received his money, but I doubt if anyone dared to follow his example. Alexander's patience and his treasury were limited.

God, on the other hand, has this world and the next to give if we take the time to ask in faith and love. Let's not hold back from asking for what we really need, because He really can supply it.

"Until now you have not asked for anything in my name. Ask and you will receive, and your joy will be complete."

(John 16:24)

Monday – **February 20**

I'VE woken up early,
I don't know just why –
The sun is still sleeping,
So why shouldn't I?
And yet I'm not sorry
If truth must be told,
To have these few moments
Before life takes hold.
For here 'neath my duvet
It's comfy and calm,
The bed is so cosy;
The silence is balm.
So till the alarm clock
Commences to shout
I'll snuggle back down
And enjoy my time out!

Margaret Ingall

Tuesday – **February 21**

WHEN John Newton wrote "Amazing Grace" he was a clergyman in Warwickshire and he could hardly have foreseen that Native American Cherokees would be singing a version of it 70 years later.

Marched along the thousand mile "Trail of Tears" to their new reservation, they sang the hymn so often in tribute to the dead they left on the way that it became a part of their folklore.

But if something touches the human soul, it has the power to touch every human soul, no matter where, no matter when and no matter in what situation.

Amazing, isn't it? But Grace is Grace – and always will be.

Her Little Lambs

Wednesday – **February 22**

ANNIE is forever bustling here and there. She always has something to do, whether it is for herself, her family, her friends or total strangers, and she likes it that way. She is especially good at crafts, baking and crochet.

"I like to follow the example of the little fellow who sits on my mantelpiece," Annie told the Lady of the House one winter afternoon.

Her bewilderment must have been obvious because Annie laughed and then explained. "The clock. He passes time in the best possible way – by keeping his hands busy!"

Thursday – **February 23**

NORMAN Vincent Peale became famous for encouraging people to think positively through his best-selling inspirational books. I'd like to share one of his quotes with you that has often lifted my spirits during challenging times:

"Become a possibilitarian. No matter how dark things seem to be or actually are, raise your sights and see possibilities – always see them, for they're always there."

Friday – **February 24**

ACTRESS Doris Day is famous for her sunny disposition and she had this advice that echoed the title of her 1960 film "Please Don't Eat The Daisies":

"We plant seeds that will flower as results in our lives, so best to remove the weeds of anger, avarice, envy, and doubt ..."

Oh, and please don't eat the daisies!

Saturday – **February 25**

ALL I know about Harold B. Melchart is that he seems to have been a wise man with a fondness for mountains. We might not always reach the summits, but even a life spent on the low ground can seem like something of an uphill struggle at times. So a little mountaineering wisdom might not go amiss!

"Live your life each day as you would climb a mountain," Melchart wrote. "An occasional glance toward the summit keeps the goal in mind, but many beautiful scenes are to be observed from each new vantage point."

Something for all of us to remember as we make our way through a new year.

Sunday – **February 26**

READING about the pioneering days of the American West, our friend John learned the city of Independence in Missouri was known as "The Queen of Trails," because of the number of routes west accessible from there.

Thousands of people loaded everything they could lift into their covered wagons and set off in search of a better life. Almost as soon as they left Independence, however, the trail would be littered with items flung out of the wagons to lighten the load.

Those trails to a better life were not easy, and neither is our path to eternal life. Worldly goods might be necessary, but too many can weigh you down and the wise traveller knows they don't compare to the prize at the end of the trail.

"It is easier for a camel to go through the eye of a needle than for a rich man to enter the kingdom of God." (Mark 10:25)

Monday — **February 27**

JIM is just back from a month's holiday in Australia. While he was there, he came across a little piece of aboriginal wisdom – he applied it to his holiday and now he plans to apply it to the rest of his life.

It says: "We are all visitors to this time, this place. We are just passing through. Our purpose here is to observe, to learn, to grow, to love. . . and then we return home."

Tuesday — **February 28**

GRAEME has a decidedly off-beat way of looking at life, so I wasn't too surprised when he said one day, "Aren't trees and hedges a lot like people?"

However, I was a bit bewildered at first.

"Well, some stand separate and tall and have an individual dignity, while others grow close and intermingle and get their strength from the group – but it takes both types to make the whole picture," he continued.

Now, that's something to think about today!

Wednesday — **February 29**

IS there someone in your life who never turns down a request for help, no matter where it comes from? As this Korean proverb puts it so aptly: "The great river refuses no stream."

Each great river starts off small, but it carries the water of many other streams to the sea, and in doing so it becomes bigger. So it is with people who don't hesitate to take on another's burden – they become bigger, greater people in the process.

March

Thursday — ***March 1***

I'M sure many readers will have heard of the American novelist Henry James, but perhaps few will know anything about his older brother. William James followed a distinguished career of his own, but in medicine. However, having come across a collection of thoughts ascribed to him, I can see that Henry was not the only one gifted with insight into human nature:

"Act as if what you do makes a difference. It does."

"Believe that life is worth living and your belief will help create the fact."

"If you want a quality, act as if you already had it."

"Let everything you do be done as if it makes a difference."

Surely an excellent prescription for a fulfilling life.

Friday — ***March 2***

EVERY autumn our old friend Mary plants several clumps of snowdrop bulbs. Last September, she planted some single-flowered snowdrops, which have a delicate, sweet smell of honey.

James Montgomery, a Scottish poet, called snowdrops in all their simplicity of ice-white flowers and fresh green leaves, "the morning star of flowers". Mary now has many "morning stars" in full bloom lasting into the earliest days of March.

A small festival of snowdrops for her and her friends to enjoy, a display which promises that a new year is moving steadily towards the gates of spring.

Saturday – **March 3**

ALL things are for the best. Could you live by these words? Bernard Gilpin tried to. But when, in the sixteenth century, he was summoned to London to be tried for heresy and faced probable execution, his optimism must have been tested.

When, on the way, he broke his leg, and an onlooker asked if all was still for the best, he must have gritted his teeth and struggled with considerable pain and discomfort before saying, "I still believe so."

His broken leg slowed him down considerably, and during the delay the monarch he had offended died. He was a free man again.

We just never know … and isn't that sometimes a good thing?

Sunday – **March 4**

MAGGI Hambling is a painter and sculptor who produced a series of works based on the North Sea. In an interview she explained how the sea had always fascinated her and as a child she used to wade into it and talk to it. Now, as she gets older, she finds she talks to the sea less – and listens more.

Maggi's experience mirrors the one many of us have with God. As children we pray for things we would like from Him. As we get to know Him better and trust Him more we tend to stop asking what He can do for us and ask what we might do for Him.

"Give ear and come to me; hear me, that your soul may live. I will make an everlasting covenant with you, my faithful love promised to David."

(Isaiah 55:3)

Monday – **March 5**

COUNTLESS children have good reason to be grateful to Louis Pasteur. His method of sterilising milk meant they could get its benefit without worrying about the bacteria it carried. But the respect, it seems, would work both ways.

Pasteur said, "When I approach children they inspire in me two sentiments – tenderness for what they are and respect for what they may become."

I'm sure anyone who's ever spent time with children would know exactly what he meant.

Tuesday – **March 6**

IT isn't always easy
When days slide by so fast:
To juggle plans for future,
With pledges to the past,
But here's a word of wisdom
If you will just allow –
The thing that really matters
Is simply Here and Now
So let Today flow freely –
Enjoy its spark and fizz,
The reason it's called "present"
Is present's what it is!

Margaret Ingall

Wednesday – **March 7**

MANY people are following various healthy-eating and weight-reducing diets these days and taking it all very seriously. However, I had to smile when the Lady of the House, with a straight face, said to me, "I like to follow a balanced diet. A cake in each hand!"

Thursday — ***March 8***

"FRIENDS are like ivy," said our local gardening expert, Harry. I had no idea what he meant but I waited with bated breath to see what came next.

"Well, it sticks with us no matter what the weather. It hides the rough spots and the gaps in our lives. And there comes a time, when our bricks are crumbling and we are ready to tumble down, when we realise that it is the ivy, and the ivy alone, that's holding us up."

I'll certainly cling to that thought!

Friday — ***March 9***

AN anonymous philosopher once said, "Don't treat life the way it treats you – be gentler."

Why are these words so memorable? Because they appeal to each of us to rise to the occasion, to be better than we might usually be. I know, without a doubt, that there is a better person within each of us, someone who can rise to the occasion, and can make this life a kinder, more loving experience.

Saturday — ***March 10***

FRANCES Hodgson Burnett was born in the slums of Victorian Manchester, so she knew a thing or two about empty hands. But she also had an important lesson to pass on about giving.

In her children's book, "A Little Princess", she wrote: "Though there may be times when your hands are empty, your heart is always full and you can give things out of that."

Golden Fringe

Sunday – ***March 11***

AS any archer will tell you, it's easy to miss! Your stance might be perfect. The arrow can be fitted just right with the correct amount of tension on the string. But if you take your eye off the target at the last minute, all the rest has been for nothing.

I read that the word translated from Hebrew and Greek as "sin" literally means "to miss the mark".

We might go to church and say our prayers, then at the moment of temptation we miss the mark. What do we do then? We re-focus. We keep our eyes on the target, which is Heaven with our Lord. And the next time we aim to hit that mark.

"You need to persevere so that when you have done the will of God, you will receive what he has promised." (Hebrews 10:36)

Monday – ***March 12***

THE Lady of the House often sees Sarah out and about early in the day. If she's not visiting friends or off to the shops, she'll be taking her grandsons to school. And if she doesn't see her coming, the Lady of the House often overhears her singing to herself.

She asked Sarah about this one day.

"Oh, it's just something my mother used to say," she replied. "She'd say, 'Start off your day with a song and it's sure to end on a good note'."

"Does it work?" the Lady of the House asked.

"It might," Sarah said with a smile. "If you didn't keep interrupting me. Even better, you could join in and see for yourself."

So she did, and it *did* make a difference!

Tuesday — ***March 13***

WE'VE all heard the expression "count to 10" when it comes to controlling our feelings, but our friend Joanne heard of a novel twist on the theme from her brother. He was on a training course for work and the subject under discussion was "teamwork".

"Before you lose your temper at some fault of a team-mate," the trainer had said, "make a point of counting to ten. That is, 10 faults of your own. See if your team-mate looks so bad then."

Wednesday — ***March 14***

HOW many of us think that we know exactly how to make the world a better place but prefer to wait for someone else to actually do it? Almost all, I suspect!

Now next time I'm tempted to wait for "Them" to sort something out, I hope I'll remember what Mahatma Gandhi once said: "You must be the change you wish to see in the world."

Inspiring words, ones we should all keep in mind.

Thursday — ***March 15***

WE often talk about the value of friends in times of trouble or need, but what about the sheer joy of having a friend when life is good? American President Thomas Jefferson was not one to let this blessing slip by unnoticed.

"Friendship is precious," he wrote, "not only in the shade but also in the sunshine of life; and thanks to a benevolent arrangement of things, the greater part of life is sunshine."

Friday – ***March 16***

APOLOGIES are usually the words people least want to say and often they have to be summoned with a deep breath. Perhaps we would be keener to utter those healing words if we thought of them the way author Margaret Lee Runbeck did.

"Apology," she wrote, "is a lovely perfume; it can transform the clumsiest moment into a gracious gift."

Saturday – ***March 17***

THERE is no such thing as a life without problems. The trick is, though, not to get so wrapped up in the occasional passing worry that we forget to appreciate all we have going for us.

As the well-known crime writer Agatha Christie said: "I like living. I have sometimes been acutely miserable, racked with sorrow, but through it all I still know quite certainly that to be alive is a grand thing!"

Sunday – ***March 18***

A FRIEND who travelled with Mother Teresa told of a little habit she had when she was talking to someone about the good work that still needed to be done. She would gently take the person's hand then touch the tips of the fingers, allocating each one a quiet word.

The words were: "Jesus. Did. It. For. You."

"For we are God's workmanship, created in Christ Jesus to do good works, which God prepared in advance for us to do."

(Ephesians 2:10)

Nearly There

Monday — **March 19**

THE Lady of the House and I received a cheerful letter from our friend Gillian one day. In it she wrote this, besides promising us a visit soon:

"We had a wonderful day out recently when we went to a Spring Garden Open Day. It was a bright sunny day, and the garden was as pretty as a picture with its white dovecote, flowering trees and its wild garden beside a little stream. This garden was a peaceful, green place jewelled with small daffodils, crocuses and dog's tooth violets. Doesn't a new spring day in all its vitality and beauty lift the heart?"

It is a seasonal reminder that the winds of March and showers of April "bring forth May flowers". William Morris, the Victorian poet, wrote of March in his "Earthly Paradise", which was devoted to the months of the year:

Stayer of the Winter, art thou here again?
O welcome, thou that bringst the Summer nigh.

Tuesday — **March 20**

LIKE the ripples on a pool
Which gradually increase,
So the seeds of kindness spread
Once they find release.
A caring heart, a cheery smile,
A ready listening ear,
Little acts and deeds of love
And words that are sincere —
All help to oil the wheels of life
As we go on our way,
So act upon that loving thought
And make somebody's day.

Kathleen Gillum

Wednesday — **March 21**

ARE there any benefits to growing older? Some people don't think so but I don't agree. How could you work hard all those years, make all those mistakes, learn all those lessons, have your heart broken – and healed again – and not have something to show for it? These words from the Talmud are worth thinking about:

"For the unlearned," it says, "old age is winter; but for the learned it is the season of the harvest."

Thursday — **March 22**

ACCORDING to a Country and Western song, "Bad news travels like a wildfire, good news travels slow". There is a lot of truth in these words.

Why is it that so often people talk about the bad news, the disasters and tragedies?

Acts of courage and generosity are taking place around us every day. Let's talk about them for a change and we might begin to see the world in a different light.

Friday — **March 23**

THERE'S a wonderfully descriptive Spanish proverb that says, "Habits are first cobwebs, then cables". In other words, things that start off unimportant and insubstantial can soon become very influential. But habits can be good, as well as bad, and cables can support as well as tie down.

So, let's take a fresh look at the habits in our own lives and those we are instilling in the next generation. If they are good let's make them stronger but if they aren't, then let's brush them away like ... well, like cobwebs!

Parade of Pink

Saturday – **March 24**

HAVE you ever wondered why military personnel salute each other? Apparently it comes from the days of knights in armour. A knight who wasn't looking for a fight would raise his visor to show his face and thus clearly indentify himself as a friend.

What has that to do with modern life, you might wonder. Well, how many of us walk through life wearing guarded expressions? Our armour is well and truly in place.

Let's try, when we meet a new acquaintance or an old friend – or maybe even someone we're not so fond of – to mentally raise our visor, show who we really are, and salute them with a smile!

Sunday – **March 25**

FOR an experiment, Joshua Bell, one of the world's leading violinists, dressed in jeans and a baseball cap and went busking in the Washington subway. The former child prodigy played a Stradivarius worth four million dollars but only made a little over 32 dollars. Thousands of commuters walked past without a second glance.

But a hidden camera spotted one man looking back from the escalator. By the time he reached the top, the man was entranced and he stayed there till the music finished. He didn't recognise Joshua Bell, he only knew he was in the presence of a great talent.

God works amongst us every day and, like the man on the escalator, we need to be prepared to find the extraordinary in ordinary situations.

"He was in the world, and though the world was made through him, the world did not recognise him."

(John 1:10)

Monday — **March 26**

THE famous frontiersman and explorer of the American West Daniel Boone was in his eighties when he wrote to his sister-in-law describing his faith and the code he lived by. He summed it all up by saying he had always tried to "do all the good to my neighbours and myself that I can and trust in God's mercy for the rest."

Daniel Boone expressed to perfection a way of life to which we can all aspire.

Tuesday — **March 27**

AUTHOR LM Montgomery in "Anne Of Avonlea", speaking through her central character, says: "The nicest and sweetest days are not those on which anything very splendid or wonderful or exciting happens but those that bring simple little pleasures, following one another softly, like pearls slipping off a string."

A life which has more than a few days like that is blessed indeed!

Wednesday — **March 28**

SOMETIMES, as hard as it might be to believe, you can have so much to do that you never get anything done. We've all had days like these and they are often memorable for all the wrong reasons.

Well, here's some advice from a busy person, Lady Stella Reading, who founded the Women's Voluntary Service, which went on to become that much-loved organisation, the Women's Royal Voluntary Service.

She recommended prioritising, or as she put it, "The whole point about getting things done is knowing what to leave undone."

Thursday — **March 29**

SOME of us aspire to lofty ideals, while others prefer to live more practical lives. Philanthropist Hannah More, managed to combine the options.

She took a virtue and pointed out the practical benefits of it when she wrote: "Forgiveness is the economy of the heart. It saves the expense of anger, the cost of hatred and the waste of spirit."

Friday — **March 30**

ARE you facing a task that appears to be going nowhere? Take heart, for throughout history people faced all kinds of obstacles, but still overcame them.

And if we can't solve everything at once, let's keep in mind these wise words from St Francis of Assisi who advised: "Start by doing what's necessary; then do what's possible; and suddenly you are doing the impossible."

And look how much *he* achieved!

Saturday — **March 31**

WE want from friendship
All those things,
True understanding
Always brings.
The special thoughts
That mean so much,
Consideration's gentle touch.
But we in turn
Must effort make,
To give as much,
As we would take.

Elizabeth Gozney

April

Sunday – ***April 1***

THANKSGIVING should be considerably more than the well-known American celebration in November. Let me explain.

Henry Frost wrote of his time as a missionary in China: "I had received sad news from home and deep shadows had covered my soul. I prayed but the darkness did not vanish. Then I saw these words on the wall of a mission: *Try Thanksgiving*. I did, and in a moment every shadow was gone, not to return."

"Give thanks to the Lord, for He is good; His love endures forever." (Chronicles I, 16:33)

Monday – ***April 2***

AN archaeologist was talking about early man. She believed, she said, that many of the tribes were not as savage as generally thought.

She spoke about the discovery of ancient human bones that had been damaged, or even broken, yet had healed completely. "This could not have happened if the sufferer had not received help from others during the healing process," she commented.

"Then there is the evidence of early medicines. Plants and roots were used to cure all sorts of diseases and injuries. They looked after the sick in their community."

It is wonderful to think that caring for one another started in the very dawn of human history.

Tuesday – ***April 3***

JMW TURNER painted some of the most glorious landscapes in British art. At first his Impressionist style offended many people, but he gradually won them over and today his colourful studies of sea and sky are among the nation's finest treasures.

It is believed he was short-sighted, and this forced him to paint as he did, without detail.

While other painters might have given up in the face of such adversity, Turner triumphed over it. And for me, knowing this, makes his pictures all the more beautiful.

Wednesday – ***April 4***

EASTER LILIES

WE forget all about them
In the year's darkness, in the long winter

Without a sound they are there one morning
A kind of sunlight grown from the ground

As if some call had woken them
From the underworld of their sleep

Out into the middle of March
To Easter the earth with their heads

Flapped and flayed by the wind
Broken yolks splashing the air

All that we hoped for
An answer to prayer.

Kenneth Steven

Thursday – **April 5**

I READ that ironing has been voted the most boring household chore. But does it have to be? I recall a conversation with an old lady I knew who was often ironing when the Lady of the House called.

"I love it," she told her. "When I smooth out all the creases I'm smoothing away all my troubles. By the time I'm finished they will all be gone!"

Isn't that a positive way to look at a humdrum task?

Friday – **April 6**

DOUGLAS has what he believes is an important job: he is a careers guidance teacher in a large secondary school.

"I encourage the pupils to be ambitious," he told me. "And not just for material success. The message I give them is, 'Of course it's fine to make a living but even better to make a life'."

Inspiring words for young folk as they prepare to go out into the world.

Saturday – **April 7**

"WE'LL meet again . . . " What better words can you have when your loved one has gone away?

The speaker was Dame Vera Lynn talking, of course, about the song that brought hope and comfort to thousands during the Second World War.

Unlike many of the wartime performers, she never lost her place in the hearts of the public and her songs lived on. In 2009, aged 92, she was the oldest performer to have a number one album.

Soon after, she received a Lifetime Achievement award, richly deserved.

Sunday — ***April 8***

IT'S Easter morning.
There is fresh green on the maple
and a new blush on the crocuses.
A robin sings on my lawn;
she fills her tiny breast and cries,
He lives!
Each blade of grass kneels in the wind
and whispers,
He lives!
The rose bushes
exhale perfume
and the cedars
brim with spice
and sigh,
He lives!
And sparrows write He lives! upon the sky.
The earth is keeping Easter in its heart –
and so shall I.

Rachel Wallace-Oberle

Monday — ***April 9***

EASTER is a real mixture. Old traditions mix with the new, fun for children runs alongside spiritual joy for adults, yet joining it all together is one truth.

I don't know who wrote these Easter wishes, but they surely sum up this time of year perfectly:

Blessed are those to whom Easter is not a hunt
but a find;
Not a greeting but a proclamation;
Not an outward fashion but an inward grace;
Not a day . . . But an eternity.

Light In The Darkness

Tuesday — *April 10*

WHAT'S your favourite early morning smell? There are a good many to choose from, whether it's the fragrance of fresh, damp air or the enticing aromas of fresh coffee or sizzling bacon! Now, here's one I hadn't thought of:

I love the sweet smell of dawn –
Our unique daily opportunity to smell time,
To smell opportunity –
Each morning being a new beginning.

These words come from Emma Woodhull-Bache – and I think her choice may be the best one of all!

Wednesday — *April 11*

WHEN Jack graduated from divinity college, the top student of his year, his friends expected to see him soon in the pulpit of a large and well-off church. "He will go far," they said.

But Jack had other ideas and today he is ministering to the people of a large housing estate, notorious for its high crime rate and social problems.

When asked why he chose this path he replied: "I wanted to care for the last, and least and the lost and I've found them here."

God bless Jack and his flock.

Thursday — *April 12*

THE best advice often comes short and sweet, and here are some words of wisdom from novelist Henry James to prove my point: "Three things in human life are important. The first is to be kind. The second is to be kind. The third is to be kind."

No, I can't think of anything more to add, either!

Friday – ***April 13***

HAVE you ever noticed how it's often the people who have the least who give the most? It's also the folk who have had the most knocks in life who frequently help others up.

I'm sure you know exactly what I mean because you have no doubt had your own hard times. But don't problems seem to make you a wiser person in the end?

There's a Mexican proverb that seems to sum it all up perfectly: "You need to learn to lose before you can play the game properly."

Saturday – ***April 14***

IF everything you do seems to be going nowhere here are some insightful words by Jacob Riis to keep in mind:

"When nothing seems to help, I go and look at a stone cutter hammering away at a rock, perhaps a hundred times, without so much as a crack showing in it. But at the one hundred and first blow it will split in two and I know it was not that last blow that did it, but all that had gone before."

Sunday – ***April 15***

THESE days when someone is described as submissive, it often implies they are weak or ineffectual. But the Latin "submission" means "under a mission" or "one who acts under orders". Submissive Christians are neither weak nor ineffectual – they are people on a mission.

"He said to them, 'Go into all the world and preach the good news to all creation'." (Mark 16:15)

Monday – **April 16**

WHEN something comes out of the blue to worry us, be it health, work or family related, it can often be difficult to see beyond the present moment – to catch sight of a positive future.

The Indian poet Rabindranath Tagore wrote: "I thought that my voyage had come to an end at the last limit of my power, that provisions were exhausted and the time had come to take shelter in silent obscurity.

"But I find Thy will knows no end in me and when old words die out on the tongue new melodies break forth from the heart; and where the old tracks are lost new country is revealed with its wonders. Suddenly I knew that while I might be powerless, God is not."

We don't know what the future holds, but we do know it is in good hands.

Tuesday – **April 17**

I WISH for you a smoother path,
All problems left behind,
A little joy, a lighter heart,
A calm and quiet mind.

I wish you hope and happiness
Along the path you tread,
And gentle, sweet tranquillity
To fill the days ahead.

I wish you peace to soothe the soul,
Each doubt and fear dispel,
And love which grows and knows no bounds
And whispers, "All is well."

Iris Hesselden

Wednesday — ***April 18***

"AH, the good old days!" Which of us hasn't whiled away a pleasant half hour – or longer – in the past, enjoying golden moments again for the umpteenth time? We should perhaps be looking ahead, getting on with the business of life, but a little wool-gathering never hurt anyone and it is so very pleasant.

The 18th-century romantic writer Jean Paul Richter must have agreed when he wrote, "Recollection is the only paradise from which we cannot be turned out."

Thursday — ***April 19***

ARE you feeling snowed under? Sometimes even the most organised of us can find that life is getting a little out of hand, so if you happen to be juggling all kinds of commitments right now, then I have some excellent advice from Albert Einstein:

"Three rules of work: out of clutter find simplicity; from discord find harmony; in the middle of difficulty lies opportunity."

So take a deep breath and – good luck!

Friday — ***April 20***

HOW did you feel when you woke up this morning? Perhaps we could all take a leaf out of the writer Arnold Bennett's book. Here is what he said:

"You wake up in the morning, and lo! Your purse is magically filled with 24 hours of the magic tissue of the universe of your life. No-one can take it away from you."

What an inspiring thought to begin the day!

Saturday – ***April 21***

CHARLES Kingsley, author of the children's classic "The Water Babies", reminds us that it is "a blessed thing for any man or woman to have a friend". He also points out that friendships often need work but they are usually worth the effort.

"If we have had the good fortune to win such a friend," he wrote, "let us do anything rather than lose them. We must give and forgive: live and let live. If our friends have faults we must bear with them.

"We must hope all things, believe all things, endure all things, rather than lose that most precious of earthly possessions – a trusty friend. And a friend once won need never be lost, if we will only be trusty and true ourselves."

Sunday – ***April 22***

THE words in this popular prayer are ascribed t St Richard, Bishop of Chichester in the 13th century, man of strong character, a scholar who was renowned for energy and kindness.

Thanks be to Thee, my Lord Jesus Christ
For all the benefits Thou hast given me
For all the pains and insults Thou hast borne
for me.
O most merciful Redeemer, friend and brother
May I know Thee more clearly.
Love Thee more dearly,
Follow Thee more nearly,
Day by day.

It is, of course, familiar to us more musically thes days, the words having been adapted for the song, "Day By ay" by Stephen Schwartz in the musical "Godspell".

Monday – **April 23**

BRENDA was in a cheerful mood when the Lady of the House called to deliver a bunch of flowers for her birthday. "I've just opened a card from my niece," she told me. "The last time we saw each other, I'd been going through some old photos, and grumbling about how old I was looking. So it really cheered me up to see that she had written these lines by John Donne in her card:

"No spring, nor summer beauty hath such grace,
As I have seen in one autumnal face."

Good words to remember when we don't feel quite as youthful as once we did!

Tuesday – **April 24**

EB White, the author of children's classics "Stuart Little" and "Charlotte's Web", once wrote: "I rise in the morning torn between a desire to improve the world and a desire to enjoy the world. This makes it hard to plan the day."

I'm sure he knew only too well that if you set out each day without a plan, but with an open heart, the choice won't be one or the other. You will not only make the world better but you'll enjoy doing it as well!

Wednesday – **April 25**

ARE you thinking of embarking on a new venture, but feeling a little nervous about it? Well, Mark Twain offered this advice: "Twenty years from now you will be more disappointed by the things you didn't do than by the ones you did do. So throw off the bowlines. Sail away from the safe harbour. Catch the Trade Winds in your sails. Explore. Dream. Discover."

Enjoy your travels!

Thursday — ***April 26***

A RETIRED social worker friend told me about the biggest compliment he ever received. A troubled young man had spent a long time getting back on to the right track and one day came to say goodbye before going off to take up a good job and a new life.

As they shook hands the young man had said to him: "I like me when I am with you."

He has remembered these words ever since. Now ask yourself, who would you say them to – and who could you bring out the best in, so that they might say them to you?

Friday — ***April 27***

IF you happen to be feeling a little jaded today, here's one sound piece of advice to keep in mind: "Teach this triple truth to all – a generous heart, kind speech, and a life of service and compassion are things which renew humanity."

Buddha

Saturday — ***April 28***

I LEANED on George's garden fence, reluctant to disturb his peace. He was kneeling on a cushion beside a flower bed with a handful of seeds he was about to plant, but he seemed lost in thought. He looked up when he at last realised I was there.

"I was trying to remember some words from the East," he said. "Happiness held is the seed . . ."

". . . And happiness shared is the flower," I finished the quote.

George laughed and carried on planting happiness. I left, already looking forward to the flowers.

Tranquillity

*Sunday — **April 29***

IF you visit the Louvre Museum in Paris you might be surprised by the number of people sketching or copying the paintings on the walls, but in fact the Louvre has always encouraged artists and students to copy their precious masterpieces. After all, how better to develop artistic skills than by copying the brush strokes of painters like Renoir, Michaelangelo and Da Vinci?

Copying the masters seems to work for painting, but exactly where would you look if you wanted to polish up on your love, grace and faith? Which Master would you decide to choose then?

"Be imitators of God, therefore, as dearly loved children, and live a life of love, just as Christ loved us and gave Himself up for us." (Ephesians 5:1-2)

*Monday — **April 30***

MOST people have heard of Roy Rogers, the singing cowboy. His large number of film exploits have become legendary, but more important to him was his faith. The money he earned as a film star helped to support a large number of charities. Passing on what God had given to him, was how Roy described it.

However, you could be excused for thinking that more had been taken from Roy than he was ever given. His first wife and three of his children died tragically, yet his faith grew stronger.

"If there were no valleys along the trail," he explained, "there would be no mountains either. The valleys are where I learn how small I am, the mountaintop is where I see how great He is."

May

Tuesday – **May 1**

THE Roman poet Ovid said: "Take rest, a field that has rested gives a beautiful crop."

Often we underestimate the benefits of relaxation. Achievement and ambition seem much more admirable than stopping to smell the roses.

When you find yourself needing a break from the hustle and bustle of life, refresh your mind and body by taking a long walk. Meditate or read a book. Stop and chat to a friend. Write a poem or a letter. Sleep in on a Saturday morning.

Take a little rest, however you choose to make time for yourself. Today, slow things down and tomorrow you might find that what you give the world is more meaningful.

Wednesday – **May 2**

YOU can't beat a good conversation with a friend. It's an excellent way of getting to know new acquaintances, too, and a delightful way of passing time with familiar folk.

That said, the art of conversation is not as simple as it might seem and it's very easy to get wrong. That's why I try to bear in mind these words passed to me by a friend who had, on occasion, rambled on a bit: "Lord, fill my mouth with worthwhile stuff, and nudge me when I've said enough!"

Thursday — **May 3**

OUR friend and near neighbour Tom told me that he was moving. He'd been through a particularly challenging time and felt that he needed to relocate to get away from it all and to find a fresh perspective.

"Where are you going?" I asked.

"The city of Happiness," he replied.

"Where's that?" I enquired, intrigued.

"In the state of Mind," Tom smiled as he walked away.

I'd say he was halfway there already – and he hadn't even left town!

Friday — **May 4**

A FRIEND from abroad was visiting and the Lady of the House and I took him on one of our favourite walks. We met several fellow walkers and I stopped to pass the time of day.

"Do you know all these people?" Frank asked.

"No," I told him. "I've never seen them before."

He looked amazed. "We would never dream of speaking to complete strangers like that."

I hope he took the idea home with him!

Saturday — **May 5**

GOING away on holiday can be rather a busy, almost stressful time. There can be traffic problems, delays for trains, planes and boats.

That's why, as she gets her suitcase out, our old friend Mary says, "I always remember to pack my patience!"

Sound advice indeed.

Sunday – **May 6**

JOHN Wesley became a great preacher and a truly humble man, but in his younger days he showed a touch of arrogance. Talking to a porter while attending Oxford University, he learned that this happy and thankful man lived an impoverished life. He had one change of clothes and didn't even own a bed.

Sarcastically, Wesley asked him, "And what else do you thank God for?"

"Well," came the reply, "I thank Him for life and being, a heart to love Him and, above all, a constant desire to please Him!"

Young Wesley walked away subdued and wiser, with a new insight into life.

"Continue to live in Him, rooted and built up in Him, strengthened in the faith as you were taught, and overflowing with thankfulness." (Colossians 2:6)

Monday – **May 7**

THE nineteenth-century English novelist Arnold Bennett told of a secretary who worked at his publishing firm. Everyone knew she was the best secretary in town and she had been offered higher wages to go elsewhere but she had decided to stay in her post.

Eventually Mr Bennett asked the secretary what her secret was. She said it was more to do with her boss than with her. He was a man who noticed even the smallest efforts she made – and never failed to appreciate them! His appreciation made her want to do even better in return.

There are many ways to get the best from people, but I agree with Mr Bennett. None of them beats a smile and a sincere thank you.

Tuesday — **May 8**

I'D never heard of a "hilltop hour" but, thinking about it later, I've been lucky enough to know quite a few and I hope you have, too. They are those times when all your hard work pays off, when things are just right and all seems well with the world.

What is it that makes these moments so special? Hard as it might be to realise, we have the bad times to thank for making the good times so good.

As Helen Keller put it so well: "The hilltop hour would not be so wonderful if there were no dark valleys to traverse."

Wednesday — **May 9**

A CORRESPONDENT sent me this verse written by the nineteenth-century American poet and man of letters James Russell Lowell and I'd like to share it with you today:

True love is but a humble, low-born thing,
And hath its food served up in earthen ware;
It is a thing to walk with, hand in hand,
Through the everydayness of this workday world.

The author surely understood the nature of true love and the part it plays in our lives. Besides being a well-known man of letters, James Russell Lowell was also in the course of his busy life a professor and the American Ambassador to Britain and Spain.

Thursday — **May 10**

OUR neighbour Simon's clergyman has a keen sense of humour. When attendance dropped significantly during an especially glorious spell of summer weather, he posted this question on the church's outdoor sign:

What's missing from CH _ _ CH? U R!

Friday – **May 11**

WILLIAM Wordsworth was probably talking about putting those first words on paper to create another poem like "Daffodils".

Walt Disney had bigger projects in mind. After all, he had films to produce, with all the money, staff and processes involved. However, both men gave remarkably similar advice about getting things done.

Disney said: "The way to get things started is to stop talking and start doing." Wordsworth was even more succinct: "To begin," he wrote, "begin."

Excellent advice, which I will try to take on board right after another cup of tea!

Saturday – **May 12**

HOPE, dream, remember
These gifts lie deep within,
And when the days are stormy
Let inner peace begin.
Hope can light the darkest night
Don't let it slip away,
Hold fast to dreams and keep them safe
For dreams can light the day.

Remember all those happy times
The things you used to do,
And cherish all your memories
For they are precious too.
With hopes and dreams and memories
To lift your heart each day,
You'll face tomorrow cheerfully,
Step lightly on your way.

Iris Hesselden

Rest Awhile

Sunday – ***May 13***

OPRAH Winfrey is well known and her Oprah's Angels network raises a huge amount of money for charities around the world.

But her childhood promised none of this. She was raised in rural poverty before her family moved to an inner city ghetto. So, what happened?

"For every one of us that succeeds," Oprah said, "it's only because somebody showed them the way out. The light doesn't always have to be in your family: for me it was teachers and school."

We can't all be world famous, but each of us has it in us to be a "light" that shows the way. When Jesus spoke again to the people, he said: "I am the light of the world. Whoever follows me will never walk in darkness, but will have the light of life."

(John 8:12)

Monday – ***May 14***

OUR friend Gladys loves flowers. She has pots of begonias and geraniums on every windowsill, bowls of roses on tables, clouds of daffodils that seem to float across her front lawn every spring – and a garden overflowing with every bloom imaginable.

I once commented on her green fingers and, with a laugh, she shared with me a quote by Ron Atchison: "Did you know . . . that when you walk past a flower, whether it be in somebody's garden or on a vacant hillside, the flower will always smile at you.

"The most polite way to respond, I've been told, is to cheerfully return the smile."

Tuesday — ***May 15***

IF one of Elizabeth Beresford's children had not mispronounced a London place name some famous story characters would never have been born. She had taken her family to Wimbledon Common and one of them kept calling it "Wombledon".

The name sparked off an idea in the writer's head and back home she settled down to work. She wrote a book about a family of little, long-nosed creatures who lived in burrows and kept the Common free of litter.

The Wombles became national favourites and as well as entertaining, they taught us to be tidy and care for the countryside.

Wednesday — ***May 16***

THE conductor André Previn told the late, great comedian Eric Morecambe one day that he was playing all the wrong notes on the piano. Eric replied: "I'm playing all the right notes — but not necessarily in the right order!"

John Ruskin, the 19th century art critic and poet, was more serious but was perhaps more profound when he said: "All one's life is music, if we touch the right notes and in time."

Thursday — ***May 17***

CAPTAIN James Cook, the first European to make contact with the Australian continent and the Hawaiian Isles, may have come from humble origins but he didn't let that hold him back.

"Just do once what others say you can't," he wrote, "and you will never pay attention to their limitations again."

Friday – **May 18**

THIS description of happiness by Jane Porter, the 18th century Scottish novelist, will surely keep the subject well-placed in our hearts.

"Happiness," she wrote, "is a sunbeam which may pass through a thousand bosoms without losing a particle of its original ray."

Saturday – **May 19**

IT'S not often you get a laugh – and learn a lesson – out of a telling-off but our friend Jane was rather annoyed with her niece one day, a young lady full of promises but nothing yet achieved.

"It doesn't matter what you mean to do, or what you thought you might do," Jane said. "What matters to the world and the people in it is what you actually do. I know you have a heart of gold," she continued with a dead-pan expression, "but so does a boiled egg!"

Sunday – **May 20**

THE word "repent" always seems so stern, like something you would only do under the most serious of circumstances. I was intrigued to discover that the Greek word it is based on implies more of a practical second chance than a last-minute act of desperation. It means to stop travelling in the wrong direction and head the opposite way.

As we journey through this life, isn't it comforting to know that when we repent, in a very real sense we turn again towards home?

"The priest answered them, 'Go in peace. Your journey has the Lord's approval'." (Judges 18:6)

Monday – **May 21**

IT'S a do-nothing day, the sort I like best,
With no other plan than to potter and rest,
No chores to be dealt with, no schemes put in hand,
No jobs to be jobbed and no plans to be planned.
So cheerful and tranquil, I'll sit and I'll dream,
Let time trickle by like a sun-dappled stream,
Tomorrow I'll work just as hard as can be,
But till it arrives – well, today is for me!

Margaret Ingall

Tuesday – **May 22**

ROGER Babson was a businessman who once said this: "The greatest undeveloped resource of our country is faith; the greatest unused power is prayer."

A thought that's surely as applicable today as it ever was, no matter which country we call home.

Wednesday – **May 23**

IONA, off the west coast of Scotland, has been a place of pilgrimage for centuries. Ella told me about the most moving moment of her recent visit.

"From the Abbey, with others from many lands, I walked to St Columba's Bay where he first came ashore to begin preaching and spreading the Gospel. We felt close to him as together we stood and repeated these words:

May kindly Columba guide us,
To be an isle in the sea,
To be a hill on the shore,
To be a star in the night,
To be a staff for the weak."

Thursday – **May 24**

IN the space of one morning the Lady of the House met Yvonne who is a volunteer driver for a cancer charity, Tricia who makes inspirational bookmarks and Dave who cares for the gardens of several much older neighbours.

Such folk consider what they do is anything but work in the traditional sense.

These words from Bliss Carman, who was once considered Canada's "unofficial poet laureate", came to mind: "Set me a task in which I can put something of my very self, and it is a task no longer. It is joy and art."

Friday – **May 25**

ROBERT struggled in school when he was young. One day, his teachers finally discovered why – he had significant hearing loss in one ear.

One of Robert's teachers decided to spend extra time tutoring and encouraging him and, because of this remarkable teacher's kindness and dedication, Robert caught up with the rest of his class. He went on to do well in examinations and now attends university.

As Mother Teresa once said: "Kind words can be short and easy to speak, but their echoes are truly endless."

Saturday – **May 26**

IN a diary full of wisdom beyond her 14 years, Anne Frank firmly believed we all had good news inside us. "The good news," she wrote, "is you don't know how great you can be! How much you can love! What you can accomplish! And what your potential is!"

You won't find that in this morning's newspapers but, really, it should be headline news every day.

Sunday – **May 27**

JOHN ADAMS, the second President of the United States, was fond of an evening "constitutional". A friend he met on one of these walks asked, "And how is John Adams today?"

At the grand age of 90 the former President replied, "This old tenement I live in may be falling down but John Adams, sir, is very well indeed!"

There's more to you, me and John Adams than meets the eye.

"I give them eternal life and they shall never perish: no-one can snatch them out of my hand."

(John 10: 27-29)

Monday – **May 28**

WHEN weariness plucks at the heartstrings
And limbs might be fashioned of lead,
And the light which is shining on others
Can't get inside of your head.
When the ship of your dreams, having foundered
Lies wrecked on a boulder-strewn beach,
And Hope is a big, shiny bubble
Just floating away, out of reach . . .

When the warmth of the fire turns to ashes
Leaving you chilled to the bone,
Don't let despair overwhelm you,
For truly, you're never alone.
Be still, in the depths of your darkness
And wait for the silence to sing,
Then know an uplifting enfolding,
And feel the soft touch of a wing.

Tricia Sturgeon

Shelter From
The Storm

Tuesday — **May 29**

JEREMY Taylor, who was once described as "the Shakespeare of the pulpit", believed that love was "friendship set on fire".

Jeremy was born in Cambridge in 1613 and became an eloquent preacher and writer, a kind and tolerant man, he was also chaplain to Charles I and the royal army during the Civil War.

When the Royalists were defeated, Jeremy was deprived of his benefice, and became a schoolmaster in Wales. Later, after Charles II became king, he became the bishop of Dromore, a Privy Councillor and Vice-Chancellor of Dublin University, but he longed for a quiet country lifestyle where he could study nature. He died in 1667, and is buried in Dromore Cathedral.

Wednesday — **May 30**

HERE are some wise words to reflect on today – and indeed every day of the year:
All people smile in the same language.

Thursday — **May 31**

"OH poor Helen," sighed The Lady of the House as she put down the phone. "Yesterday she wanted to go for a walk but the forecast suggested showers, so she stayed at home. Today she wanted to sit on her deckchair in the garden, but she couldn't relax with so much weeding to be done. You know, it's a shame that she's so good at finding Reasons-Why-Not-To."

Now, for anyone else who shares that tendency, here is a thought to remember from Annette Funicello. "Life does not have to be perfect to be wonderful."

Remember to make the most of *your* wonderful moments!

June

Friday — **June 1**

IF you've ever doubted whether good advice really can come in small packages, then how about considering these words from St Therese:

"Let us love, since our heart is made for nothing else."

Short. To the point. And perfect.

Saturday — **June 2**

I SHALL recall a spire
soaring through willows.
Cool ribbons of waterway
threaded across moist meadows.
Gaggles of geese about their business;
Funny, inquisitive ducks
performing comic turns among the reeds.
Soft speedwell arc of summer sky
framing distant hills
Whose inclines lift from a
billowing frieze of woodland.
Thoughts will retrace paths
to a quiet home, high above treetops.
Medley of chintz and garnered treasures;
Chink of tea-cups and anecdotes;
The warm haze of nostalgia and friendship
Brushing the china plates with amber light.

Joan Howes

Sunday – ***June 3***

EVERY hour, on the hour, a new guard arrives at the Tomb of the Unknown Soldier in Arlington in the United States. The guard who is being relieved speaks but three words to greet his replacement: "Orders remain unchanged," and this proud tradition has been maintained each and every year since 1937.

That absolute certainty in respect for those who died for their country is reassuring. But there are other words for those who live in this world and they have remained unchanged for more than 2000 years.

"The entire law is summed up in a single command: 'Love your neighbour as yourself'."

(Galatians 5:14)

Monday – ***June 4***

"OH dear," sighed Molly, "I do wish the world would slow down a little. It's barely New Year before we see 'Spring into Summer' advertising slogans, hardly July before 'Back to School' posters appear and then, even before the leaves start falling, we're being told to rush out and buy Christmas cards and decorations!"

Most of us can relate to Molly's feeling of being unwillingly hustled through the months at breakneck speed without a chance to pause and properly enjoy each day as it comes, taking time to draw breath and realise how special every hour is. But there's a Himalayan proverb that says, "Humans say that time passes. Time says that humans pass."

This, to me, is perfect reason to stage a small rebellion. Other people may do as they choose, but I'm making the decision to take the world at my own pace, and make sure I appreciate it.

Tuesday — ***June 5***

HE'D always fancied writing a book, but mostly he just talked about it at the kitchen table. Then one day his wife had heard enough.

"Look, I don't want to offend you," she said, "but you've been saying that for 25 years. If you were going to write a book, you'd have done it. You're never going to do it now. Old vets of 50 don't write books." So, he bought a few reams of paper and started scribbling.

Alf Wight, who became a worldwide bestseller as James Herriot, should be proof for us all that it's never too late to follow a dream!

Wednesday — ***June 6***

EACH friend represents a world in us, a world possibly not born until they arrive, and it is only by this meeting that a new world is born.

Anais Nin

Thursday — ***June 7***

THE late Robert Runcie, the Archbishop of Canterbury from 1980 to 1991, was a cricket enthusiast, and often visited Lord's when a Test Match was being played.

On one occasion, rain was making it impossible for play to take place. Dr Runcie apologised to the Pakistan High Commissioner, who was also there to watch the game, and jokingly suggested that he must have brought the rain with him.

"Your Grace," came the reply, "there is no need to apologise. In our country a guest who brings rain is an honoured and welcome guest."

Crossing The Threshold

Friday – **June 8**

THE Lady of the House came across these words written by the 16th century Dutch scholar, Erasmus, and they are surely as relevant to us today as when they were first penned:

Give light and the darkness will disappear of itself.

Saturday – **June 9**

THE success of a piece of music can be measured in many ways; how many centuries it has been around, or, if modern, how long it was at the top of the music charts, or even how wealthy it made its composer.

But imagine if the music was judged in none of those categories. Imagine if it was judged solely on the effect it had on the human soul, what would occupy the number one spot? Well, could anything beat birdsong on a summer's day?

Sunday – **June 10**

BECAUSE they are used to looking down in the direction of flowers, if a bumble bee lands in a tumbler it will bounce about the sides and the bottom, unaware it could escape by flying upwards.

And despite being incredibly nimble in the air, bats can't take off from a flat surface. They need to drop before they can rise again.

We humans often feel bogged down by our daily responsibilities, often feeling challenged by our workload and reluctant to believe we can "escape". Well, like the bee and the bat, all we need to do is look upwards.

"Your eyes will see the king in his beauty and view a land that stretches afar." (Isaiah 33:17)

Monday — ***June 11***

GEORGINA was looking at a snapshot of herself, taken as a teenager some decades ago. "I saved up for weeks to buy that dress," she reminisced. "I felt sure that if only it could be mine, I'd be happy for ever and ever."

She laughed. "It didn't work, of course, but that's the sort of thing that you only learn as you go along. Nowadays I'm wiser – I've come to see that even though nothing can guarantee permanent joy, I can still go through the day looking out for it."

As Margaret Lee Runbeck said: "Happiness is not a station you arrive at, but a manner of travelling".

Bon voyage!

Tuesday — ***June 12***

THERE'S a story told about a young clergyman relaxing on a sunny day. Lying under a large walnut tree he looks across to a neighbouring pumpkin field. Then he looks up at the tree.

For a few seconds he wonders if God is really so wise. Imagine growing huge pumpkins on such slender vines, while the majestic tree only supported such little nuts. But then a walnut landed on his head…

Just because we don't always understand, doesn't mean things aren't exactly the way they should be.

Wednesday — ***June 13***

CHEERFULNESS removes the rust from the mind, lubricates our inward machinery and enables us to do our work with fewer creaks and groans.

I don't know if it was an engineer who made that wise remark, but if it was I'll bet he was a good one!

Thursday — ***June 14***

ADVICE! We all like to give it, but few of us like to take it. Such is human nature.

Lady Mary Wortley Montagu was an 18th-century writer and aristocrat. As the wife of a politician, she was a regular at Court, a traveller in the Middle East and a friend of the women's rights movement.

Doubtless, she had plenty of good advice to offer. But she summed up, perfectly, the two opposing sides on the matter when she wrote:

"I sometimes give myself admirable advice – but I am completely incapable of taking it!"

I think many of us would sympathise, Lady Mary.

Friday — ***June 15***

HERE is a thought-provoking quote to think about today from our old friend Anon:

One of life's greatest treasures is the love that binds hearts together in friendship.

Saturday — ***June 16***

ERIC was a teacher for many years and then he was a youth leader for a while. These days he takes life a little easier, spending as much time as he can in his garden. As I passed by one day, his grandchildren were listening attentively while he explained about the different fruits and vegetables he was growing.

"Once a teacher . . ." I thought with a smile.

Someone described a teacher as a candle consuming itself to light the way for others. Shine on, Eric — and all those like him who teach in whatever way they can!

Sunday – **June 17**

IN 1909, a woman was listening to a sermon on the virtues of motherhood and she began to wonder why fathers weren't honoured in the same way. The more she thought about it, the more the idea took hold and she decided to do something about it.

Sonora Dodd enthusiastically campaigned to this end and in June 1910, in her home town of Spokane, Washington, the first Father's Day was celebrated. Gradually, this idea spread all across the United States and then became accepted worldwide.

Isn't it truly amazing what can be achieved by something that starts as a simple thought?

Monday – **June 18**

HOW did a boy raised on the pampas of South America grow up to become one of Britain's finest naturalists? William Henry Hudson loved the family ranch but books he read about the English countryside and all it had to offer inspired him and aged 33 he made the decision to set sail for Southampton.

His sketchy education did not fit him for any kind of job so, notebook in hand, he roamed the woods and fields, watching birds and animals and writing about what he observed outdoors in articles and books such as "Nature In Downland".

When he died in 1922 he was buried under a tree in Worthing Cemetery. The inscription on his stone reads: *He loved the birds and green places and the wind on the heath, and saw the brightness of the skirts of God.*

Tuesday – **June 19**

"YOU know, I never intended to become involved with the hospital fund-raisers," Debbie said one day to The Lady of the House. "But a friend had to drop out at short notice and somehow I found myself in her place, lending a hand at the summer fête.

"That was so satisfying that I agreed to assist at the next event, then the next. I made it quite clear that my involvement could only be temporary – but that was over 20 years ago!"

Debbie is not the only person to discover that helping out can be fulfilling. "The most satisfying thing in life is to have been able to give a large part of oneself to others," Pierre Teilhard de Chardin said.

Why not try doing a little something to make the world a better place?

Wednesday – **June 20**

LIKE many, Nell was born into a family that was richer in affection than in money. However, as she recalls fondly: "We were all brought up to realise that by sharing things we enhanced our pleasure, rather than diminished it."

It's a way of living that she's followed throughout a long life. On a special birthday recently, she was given a large box of chocolates – her first act was to hand it round among her friends at the local writers' circle.

"But I'm enjoying myself," she said with a smile when she was reminded to keep some for herself. "I can't think of a better way to spend time."

There's an old Greek adage that says: "Life is a gift of nature, but beautiful living is the gift of wisdom." And that's one that lasts forever.

Thursday — ***June 21***

ST CHRISTOPHER is the patron saint of travellers. It is said he was tall and strong and he used his great strength to carry travellers across a river which had no bridge.

One dark night he heard the sound of a baby crying and found it lying helplessly on the bank. He lifted it up and set off in the fast-flowing water. As he waded across, he was surprised to feel the weight on his back grow heavier with every step.

On reaching the other side and putting down his heavy load he saw that he had, in fact, carried Christ himself.

Aptly, the name Christopher means "Christ-bearer".

Friday — ***June 22***

SOMETIMES life drifts slow and steady
Undemanding, all arranged,
Then we turn – and life's off schedule,
In an instant all is changed.
Now we walk with steps uncertain,
Simple things seem hard to do,
Shadows loom to hide the future,
Every day brings challenge new.

Now's the time to gather courage
Take a breath; let trust begin,
Help will come from those around us,
Strength will come from deep within.
None of us are left unaided,
Though we falter, none need fall,
Even though we may not know them
Angels walk beside us all.

Margaret Ingall

Saturday – ***June 23***

ABBIE Graham's book "Ceremonials Of Common Days" is probably not so familiar to readers these days but the idea behind it was to find a little extra in the day; a few miracles in the ordinary. It's a way of looking at the world that gladdens my heart.

For instance, how many of us have complained about having to get up in the morning? It can be so tempting to sleep just that bit longer. This author's view was somewhat different.

"What happiness there is when I awake to find near me the gift of a morning!" she wrote.

With that attitude there surely can be no such thing as a "common day".

Sunday – ***June 24***

OUR friend John was showing his nephew the right way to use a saw. He'd been using short, jerky strokes, but this made the job harder and would quickly wear out the small part of the saw being used.

"Use the whole blade," John advised.

This reminded me of violin lessons at school. Using a similar motion with the bow all we could achieve was a tinny scratching, but when our teacher used the whole bow he achieved a much more mellow tone.

The blade or the bow isn't the length it is without good reason. Likewise, love works best when we don't just give a bit here and there, but when we give our whole heart.

"Enlarge the place of your tent, stretch your tent curtains wide, do not hold back." (Isaiah 54:2)

A Corner In Crete

Monday – **June 25**

AT the age of 51 mountaineer Vicky Jack became the first Scottish woman to climb the Seven Summits – the highest mountains on seven different continents – and the oldest British woman to scale Mount Everest.

What kept her going, training for years on end, battling blizzards, climbing in extreme temperatures, suffering altitude sickness and undertaking feats of physical endurance? The fact is she simply wanted to do it. She had made up her mind to succeed and that was that.

As Napoleon Hill says in these perceptive words: "The starting point of all achievement is desire. Keep this constantly in mind. Weak desire brings weak results, just as a small amount of fire makes a small amount of heat."

Vicky Jack achieved so much because she was determined to win through.

Tuesday – **June 26**

OUR old friend Mary's cousin sent her this little prayer and I hope these lines will bring peace and comfort to you today:

Today may there be peace within. May you trust that you are exactly where you are meant to be. May you not forget the infinite possibilities that are born of faith in yourself and others.

May you use the gifts that you have received, and pass on the love that has been given to you. May you be content with yourself just the way you are. Let this knowledge settle into your being, and allow your soul the freedom to sing, dance, praise and love.

Wednesday — **June 27**

THE wonder of the world
The beauty and the power,
The shapes of things,
Their colours, lights and shades,
These I saw.
Look ye also while life lasts.

These thoughtful lines appear inside every book by the writer, artist and illustrator Denys Watkins-Pitchford whose *nom de plume* was simply *BB*, and were familiar to his many readers who shared his enthusiasm for nature, the countryside and the outdoors.

However, the lines were not written by *BB* — they were copied by his father Walter from a gravestone in a country churchyard in the north of England.

These words by an unknown writer make a good thought for today — or any day of the week. They remind us of the precious gift of life and sight, and the miracle of our world and its creations, all things which are so easy to take for granted.

Thursday — **June 28**

I HAVE heard life described as a lot of things — a highway, a vale of tears, a box of chocolates, but I did have to pay attention when the Lady of the House described it as a "short blanket".

"We rarely get everything we want from life," she explained. "Some people will complain that the short blanket leaves their shoulders cold. So, they tug it up to their neck – and then complain their feet are cold.

"But then there are the ones who have it right — they simply appreciate having a blanket, draw their knees up and spend a very comfortable night indeed!"

Friday – **June 29**

KNOWING that Ted had recently been confined indoors due to ill health, I was pleased to pass his garden and find him outside, tending the flower beds. They were looking good, and I told him so.

"They are, aren't they?" he agreed cheerfully, pausing to lean on his spade for a moment. "And what's more, I can give you the quote that inspired me to start working on them. It's from a writer called Wendell Berry, who says:

"'One of the most important resources that a garden makes available for us is the gardener's own body. A garden gives the body the dignity of working in its own support. It is a way of rejoining the human race'."

I hope Mr Berry will forgive my pun when I call his words most fruitful!

Saturday – **June 30**

BUILD a bridge of love and light
Of kindly word and deed,
Reaching out across the dark
To those who are in need.

Build a bridge of hope and joy
Where there is sad despair,
Let the light that shines within
Show the world you care.

Build a bridge of love and peace
By trust and faith designed,
And reaching out across the earth –
A bridge for all mankind.

Iris Hesselden

Perfect Peace

July

Sunday – ***July 1***

LARRY Joe Bird came from a background of extreme poverty and went on to become one of the United States' all-time great basketball players. So how did he go from not being able to afford shoes to being inducted into the Basketball Hall of Fame?

"Well," he said, "when everything feels like an uphill struggle I just think about the view from the top."

Living the good life can be difficult at times, but when it all starts to get too much and we're tempted to backslide, just keep on going, doing what feels right – and think of that view from the top!

"Look," he said, "I see Heaven open and the Son of Man standing at the right hand of God." (Acts 7:55)

Monday – ***July 2***

JOHN Gardner held high-flying positions in the Carnegie Corporation founded by the philanthropist Andrew Carnegie, but he knew the care and attention he brought to his work could be applied equally to those who swept the road or the gardener lovingly preparing a patch of earth in the spring.

"Whoever I am," he wrote, "and whatever I am doing, some kind of excellence is within my reach."

So when you paint that fence, deal with those weeds, or make that cup of tea for a friend, do it excellently!

Tuesday — ***July 3***

I'M sure we have all heard of wealthy celebrities and their "entourages". It seems that once you have a certain amount of money, many people want a share of it and then they all want to be your closest confidant. But lose all that money and …

It's not a modern phenomenon. Queen Elizabeth I once wrote: "Prosperity provides – but adversity proves – friends."

"Friends" are easy to come by when you are rich or famous and just as easy to lose, but the true friends who will stick by you when times are hard – they're definitely the ones to keep hold of!

Wednesday — ***July 4***

"SOME people are making such thorough plans for rainy days that they aren't enjoying today's sunshine."

That perceptive observation was made by William Feather. He may have a lightweight name, but his thoughts certainly carry a load of wisdom!

Thursday — ***July 5***

WRITER John Grisham recalled a time at college when a good friend called him over to share the news that he was terminally ill. Grisham asked his friend how anyone coped with a situation like that.

"It's real simple," his friend replied, "you get things right with God and spend as much time with those you love as you can."

Life might often seem as complicated as a John Grisham novel but the important things are always "real simple" and his friend's advice is surely a sound philosophy to live by.

*Friday — **July 6***

NO-ONE could ever say that our friend, Hester, has green fingers. And though she accepts her horticultural failures with a rueful smile and listens to advice with gratitude, somehow her garden never blooms as well as it perhaps could.

Why then, do so many passers-by pause at her front gate? Well, because if Hester happens to be outside, she is always such a joy to chat to! There may be no prize-winning roses to admire, but no-one ever goes away without feeling happier for spending a few minutes in her company and sharing what's going on in their life.

"Let us be grateful to people who make us happy, they are the charming gardeners who make our souls blossom," wrote Marcel Proust.

I think he must have known someone just like Hester.

*Saturday — **July 7***

I HADN'T seen Darren for a while, so I wasn't surprised when he told me he'd been on holiday.

"A couple of friends and I decided to walk The Ridgeway long-distance footpath," he told me. "I ended up with sore feet, but I'm so glad that we didn't give way to temptation and take public transport. It meant that when we finally finished, we knew that we'd done it entirely by our own efforts."

Darren's remarks reminded me of some words from Beverly Sills, who said: "There are no shortcuts to any place worth going." I think that applies to just about every enterprise in life. It may cost us a blister or two, but at least we can stand at our destination with pride!

Sunday — **July 8**

SOME people seem beyond reaching out to, beyond all our best efforts, it seems. What can we do then? Well, just keep going!

Historians reckon that one of the most important journeys in history, the voyage of the "Mayflower" taking the Pilgrim Fathers to a new life in a new country was made at an average speed of two miles per hour! They persevered, and look at the result. So is the journey between your heart and the other person's really so far after all?

"Love is patient, love is kind. It does not envy, it does not boast, it is not proud." (Corinthians 1 13:4)

Monday — **July 9**

O OUR Father, the Sky, hear us
And make us strong.
O, our Mother, the Earth, hear us
And give us support.
O, Spirit of the East,
Send us your wisdom.
O, Spirit of the South,
May we tread your path.
O, Spirit of the West,
May we always be ready for the long journey.
O, Spirit of the North, purify us
With your cleansing winds.

Sioux Prayer.

Tuesday — **July 10**

A GOOD deed is never lost. He who sows courtesy, reaps friendship; he who plants kindness, gathers love.

St Basil

Wednesday – **July 11**

THE Lady of the House had just finished reading an interview with a well-known actor. "He says," she told me, "that even though, like many others in his profession, he's had his share of good reviews, it's always the bad ones that stick in his memory."

I think that attitude is common to a great many of us, whatever our circumstances. It's the unkind, thoughtless remarks that we tend to dwell on, while praise is perhaps dismissed as just being kind.

Let's make a resolution. If someone takes the time to offer us a compliment, let's repay the favour by accepting it with good grace. Such gifts might not come with ribbons and bows, but they are certainly presents to treasure!

Thursday – **July 12**

THE golden sandals of the sun
Steal softly on the day,
As darkened night on slippered feet
Creeps silently away.
The arrows of the morning light
Stream out across the sky,
In spears of colour, vivid, bright
Descending on from high.

The whispers of the quiet dawn
Are lost upon the breeze,
As fluted notes from feathered throats
Pour out from leafy trees.
The world wakes up and springs to life –
Shakes off its sleepy haze,
And tunes into the universe
To sing its psalm of praise.

Kathleen Gillum

Friday – ***July 13***

OH, the things that we do without thinking now that once seemed impossible! Do you, for example, remember those very first few wobbling seconds on a bike when it seemed impossible you could ever learn to balance on two tyres? Or how the coordination required to hold two knitting needles and cast on seemed like it would always be beyond you? But one day it became so simple and often when least expected!

The 17th-century cleric Thomas Fuller knew what he was talking about when he said, "All things are difficult before they are easy."

We can use his words to look back over things that are no trouble at all now, or we can consider the difficult times we may have now and know with the same certainty that easier times wait just a little way ahead.

Saturday – ***July 14***

ANGELA was reminiscing about a visit to the Farnborough Air Show. One of the highlights had been the Harrier jump jets. With an incredible roar they had hovered in front of the audience and "bowed" and "curtseyed" by dipping their nose and their tail.

But then Angela's attention was caught by a sparrow as it darted this way and that through a chain-link fence, drawing its wings in at the last split second each time. Then, ignoring the noise of engines, it sat on top of the fence and sang its heart out almost as if to say, "Thank you all, for coming to see what I can do."

It's worth remembering, with all our engineering and ingenuity that we have yet to make anything as wonderful as a tiny yet perfect sparrow.

Sunday — ***July 15***

P*EACE.* Now, how would you define that word? On reflection I can't help feeling that peace is not an absence of noise, but the presence of something far more sublime: a stillness, a deep serenity, a feeling that in the great scheme of things all is well, and forever will be. This is perhaps the reason why I like these words so much:

"The Lord bless thee, and keep thee: The Lord make his face to shine upon thee, and be gracious unto thee: The Lord lift up his countenance upon thee and give thee peace."

(Numbers 6: 24-26)

Monday — ***July 16***

"OH, a present!" Jamie exclaimed as the Lady of the House and I arrived with a parcel.

When you are young, presents are especially exciting, and both of us shared his delight at unwrapping the toy tractor.

Later, our thoughts turned to the way in which age changes our perception of what makes a memorable present. Often something as simple as a good piece of advice, a word of appreciation, or a loving hug can be worth far more than any material token.

Perhaps these words from a Hindu scripture say it all: "A gift is pure when it is given from the heart to the right person at the right time and at the right place and when we expect nothing in return."

Tuesday — ***July 17***

GOD gave you a gift of 86,400 seconds today. Have you used one to say thank you?

William Arthur Ward.

Sweet Nectar

Wednesday – ***July 18***

OUR friend, John, had been to visit his home town and, while there, happened to pass the house in which he'd grown up. "And would you believe it," he told us with mock indignation, "there's still no statue, or plaque on the wall to mark the fact I'd lived there!"

Even as we laughed, however, I couldn't help but reflect how so few people are ever likely to achieve such an honour. So, for those of us who never will, here are some words from the Greek statesman Pericles: "What you leave behind is not what is engraved in stone monuments, but what is woven into the lives of others."

It's nice to know that if we can't inspire a statue, at least we can inspire our fellow humans!

Thursday – ***July 19***

IMAGINE your husband was famous and in demand all over the world and millions of people adored him. Or imagine your wife was the author of numerous books and was frequently asked to give talks at home and abroad about them. What kind of strains do you think these demands might put on a relationship?

Ruth Bell Graham, writer and wife of evangelist Billy Graham, addressed the matter with these words:

"A good marriage," she said, "is the union of two forgivers."

Friday – ***July 20***

HERE are some memorable words from our old friend Anon., especially for this time of year when flowers are blooming everywhere: *A beautiful garden is a work of heart.*

Saturday – **July 21**

IF you should need an Angel,
Don't sigh and search the skies.
In truth, they're all about you,
Though often in disguise.

For, knowing that life's burdens
Are sometimes hard to bear,
And seeing too, that we might need
A hand, just here and there.

Some Providence took pity, and,
As though to make amends,
Scattered Angels on the earth,
And simply called them "Friends".

Tricia Sturgeon

Sunday – **July 22**

BACK from South Africa, Robert Moffat held a public meeting to encourage others to take up missionary work. Poor weather led to a small audience and he almost gave up when he saw his audience consisted almost entirely of women, because the theme of his talk came from Proverbs and was, "Unto you, oh men, I call!"

Robert Moffat persevered but was not surprised when no one came forward to volunteer at the end of the talk. Was it a wasted effort then?

Well, no, because the little boy working the organ bellows heard Moffat speak, even though he couldn't see him, and was inspired. His name was David Livingstone.

"Commit thy way unto the Lord; trust also to Him; and He shall bring it to pass." (Psalms 37:5)

Monday — ***July 23***

OUR friend Bridget never thinks anything she does is good enough. She is forever comparing herself to others who, she thinks, would achieve more than she ever could. I didn't quite know how to deal with that frame of mind, but then James stepped in.

"Why is a Stradivarius violin worth so much money? Why is a Rembrandt painting so expensive?" he asked. "Because there are only a few of them and they are each the work of a master. The same applies to you, Bridget."

Imagine her smile as it shone through. Of course, the same applies to James — and you!

Tuesday — ***July 24***

DO not anticipate trouble, or worry about what may never happen. Keep in the sunlight.

Benjamin Franklin

Wednesday — ***July 25***

BEFORE he became a General, "Stonewall" Jackson was simply Thomas Jackson, college professor.

Professor Jackson had a thankful attitude to life. "I never raise a glass of water to my lips," he wrote, "without asking God's blessing, never seal a letter without putting a word of prayer under the seal, never change my classes in the lecture room without a minute's petition for the students who go out and those who come in."

Could you fit a few more blessings and thanks into your day?

Thursday – **July 26**

IT was a constant puzzle to Gary how next door's pet rabbit kept finding new ways into his garden. As we surveyed the remnants of its latest dessert course, a couple of his strawberry plants, he sighed and smiled.

"Gardening's like that," he said. "It's a long series of defeats set against an eventual glorious victory."

I knew, he meant battles with slugs, inclement weather and all the rest, but I couldn't help thinking Gary had just summed up his life. And mine. And yours . . .

Friday – **July 27**

LORD, lend me courage to travel my way
Lord, send me purpose to deal with each day,
For life can be daunting and I'm feeling small
I fear, left alone, I might falter or fall
So walk with me, Lord, let your love hold me near
I know with your strength I can conquer all fear.

Margaret Ingall

Saturday – **July 28**

HAVE you ever felt that your life lacks opportunity? It's true that not every door can open for us – but if anyone is tempted to feel sorry for themselves, it's worth thinking about this quotation from Brother David Steindl-Rast:

"We have thousands of opportunities every day to be grateful: for having good weather, to be able to sit in such a beautiful room on such comfortable furniture, to have slept well last night, to be able to get up, to be healthy, to have enough to eat. There's opportunity upon opportunity to be grateful; that's what life is."

Sunday – ***July 29***

NO-ONE makes their way through life without coming across problems, but if you happen to be feeling so hemmed in by them that there seems no obvious solution, then it's time to remember these words from the Revelation to St John: "I have set before you an open door that no-one is able to shut."

Look for the Light and you will surely find it.

Monday – ***July 30***

SHOP-BOUGHT gifts can usually be returned or exchanged, if you keep the receipt. I don't think Thomas Aquinas had those in mind though, when he said, "A gift is, properly, an un-returnable giving."

Perhaps he had in mind the gift of a smile, the gift of time, the gift of a helping hand. We can give and receive that kind of gift every day. They cost nothing and you won't need a receipt – because no-one will want to change those gifts for anything else!

Tuesday – ***July 31***

THERE'S an old story of a king who lived in a grand castle. He was a music enthusiast and came up with the idea of stretching fine wires between the castle towers. His ambition was to build the world's biggest wind-powered harp but all he usually got from the wires was a boring hum.

Then came a storm. Thatched roofs were blown off, carts were upturned, people ran for shelter – but to the king's amazement, the wires started singing!

Isn't it ironic that it's the storms in life, the moments we think we would rather do without, that often bring out the best in people, times that make each of us sing our most beautiful song?

August

Wednesday – **August 1**

MANY and various are the ways in which people search for happiness and I smiled when I read these words on the subject by French poet Guillaume Apollinaire:

"Now and then," he wrote, "it is good to pause in our pursuit of happiness – and just be happy."

Thursday – **August 2**

OUR good friend Alison had just returned from a summer holiday in Belgium, and we were enjoying sharing her photographs of the trip. One of them was particularly intriguing, showing a high and elegant bridge on the River Meuse at Huy.

"It's the Pont Père Pire," Alison explained, "named after a Belgian monk of the Dominican order, le Père Dominique Pire. He was born in 1910, entered a Dominican monastery at Huy in 1928 and spent most of his life helping others, particularly during the Second World War. He was chaplain to the Belgian Resistance, won medals for bravery and later did so much to help refugees that he was awarded the Nobel Peace Prize.

"In fact, you'll be glad to hear that even after his death, the organisations he inaugurated, such as the University of Peace, are still in existence and carry on his wonderful work."

I think Père Pire sounds most worthy of having this impressive bridge named after him, don't you?

Set In Stone

Friday – **August 3**

FAIRGROUNDS in bygone days were quite different from the fairgrounds of today. One of the Lady of the House's favourite attractions was the Hall of Mirrors – which also served well-known novelist George Bernard Shaw as a metaphor for friendship.

"Friends," he wrote, "keep up your courage by holding up a mirror in which you can see a noble image of yourself."

With an attraction like that the old fun fair would have made a fortune!

Saturday – **August 4**

MIRACLES

BENEATH a blade of grass I saw a miracle;
A company of ants, struggling valiantly
To bring a fallen comrade home.
Among the honeysuckle I saw a miracle;
A crowd of plump, glad bumblebees,
Guiding each other to the sweetest blooms.

In the forest I saw a miracle;
Naive saplings sheltered by their leafy peers
Against the wind and sun.
At the river,
Where rocks had hurled themselves from the banks,
I saw a miracle;
A family of wrens, drinking side by side.
Never tell me the simplest, dearest things
Are not the most extraordinary,
Placed carefully to teach us
All that's precious.

Rachel Wallace–Oberle

Sunday – ***August 5***

EVERY Olympic Games begins with the torch-bearer carrying the Olympic Flame to the host city, but in Ancient Greece running with a torch was actually an event. It would take skill and planning, the weather would play a part, as would the route taken, and the first person to cross the finishing line with his torch still lit was the winner.

In life we will be subject to changes, distractions and stormy weather. It's up to us to run our race as smartly as those athletes of old did. The only difference is that when we cross that final finishing line, each and every one of us whose torch of faith still burns will be a winner.

"For this reason I remind you to fan into flame the gift of God, which is in you through the laying on of my hands."
(Timothy II 1:6)

Monday – ***August 6***

IN the days before London had proper pavements John Ruskin, the art critic, was out walking one evening accompanied by a friend.

"What disgusting stuff!" his friend said, referring to the mud beneath their boots.

Ruskin disagreed, pointing out that the mud consisted of sand: "And what is nicer than clean, white sand?" The water that made the mud soggy was the same element that made the sparkling dew-drop. And the soot that fell everywhere in London in those days was carbon which "in its crystallised perfection forms the diamond".

You might think it takes an extraordinary person to see diamonds in the mud but we can do the same if we decide to see everything in the best possible light.

Tuesday — **August 7**

"I'M at my lowest ebb." Many of us will have felt like that or known someone who felt like that. It's actually a nautical term to do with the ebb and flow of the tide.

When the tide is out your boat might well be prevented from getting into harbour by a substantial strip of sand or mud. A frustrating time for any sailor.

But there's another way of looking at it. When the tide is out as far as it can go, it's just about to start coming back in again! So, if you're feeling at your lowest ebb, try to hold on a little while longer. Things are just about to get better and you will soon be floating into a safe harbour once more.

Wednesday — **August 8**

FRIENDSHIP consists in forgetting what one gives, and remembering what one receives.

Alexandre Dumas The Younger

Thursday — **August 9**

UPON the ridge the wind blows fresh,
Salt-tanged by distant sea,
Beneath my feet the track winds on
And, oh — it sets me free!
It takes me from the dusty streets,
The noise and crush of town,
And leads me to the open hills,
The green and rolling down.
And sunlight pushes back the clouds
And skylarks' song soars high,
And all the world spreads wide and free
Beneath an endless sky.

Margaret Ingall.

Share This Moment

Friday – ***August 10***

SIR John Templeton was one of the richest men in the world. But he was also a philanthropist and deeply interested in matters of the soul. "Time" magazine listed him as a Power Giver who enabled many others to chase their dreams.

One of his favourite pieces of advice was, "an attitude of gratitude creates blessings". The next time you find yourself challenged by problems, remember Sir John's advice.

Take a moment to give thanks for all that's good in your life, then watch how an "attitude of gratitude" makes everything better!

Saturday – ***August 11***

OUR friend Grace doesn't hesitate to recommend a certain dry-cleaner she's been using for years. One day it occurred to her that other than her contact with the woman at the counter she had no idea who had actually been doing all that cleaning for so long!

I recalled these wise old words: "Don't work for recognition – but do work worthy of recognition."

Sunday – ***August 12***

IT'S a good thing to be humble but it's also important to remember that as far as God is concerned you are someone special. Winston Churchill may have managed to get the balance of modesty and pride just about right when he said, "We are all worms, but I do believe I'm a glow-worm."

"For you were once darkness, but now you are light in the Lord. Live as children of light." (Ephesians 5:8)

In His eyes we all shine!

Monday – **August 13**

LET THE SUN SHINE

IT'S strange but oh, so very true
That lots of things we've feared
Have loomed like shadows, dark and grim,
And then have disappeared.

It hasn't always been that way
But often when I dread
The breaking of a thunderstorm
The sun has shone instead!

So don't cross bridges long before
You reach the chasm wide –
It's ten to one you'll smile when once
You reach the other side!

Anon.

Tuesday – **August 14**

HAVING completed a teaching course at a large college in the middle of a busy city, Peter returned in a thoughtful mood. "I know that I've learned a lot from going there," he reflected. "But somehow, being home again makes me realise that I can discover just as much by being still and watching, as I can from talking."

His observation reminded me of something said by explorer Thor Heyerdahl: "One learns more from listening than speaking. And both the wind and the people who continue to live close to nature still have much to tell us which we cannot hear within university walls."

This leads me to the happy conclusion that wisdom can come from any direction, if we are open to receiving it.

Wednesday – **August 15**

IN Giovanni Guareschi's books, his character, Don Camillo, has a very personal relationship with Christ. The Italian priest, having fallen into one argument too many with the local Communists, is banished to a mountain retreat where his patience is soon fraying at the edges. He complains that the peace will drive him mad and "nothing ever happens".

"I don't understand you, Don Camillo," Christ answered. "Every day the sun rises and sets, every night you see billions of stars wheeling their way overhead, and all the while the grass grows and one season succeeds another. Aren't these the most important of all happenings?"

The next time we feel bored, instead of complaining, let's look around us and open our eyes!

Thursday – **August 16**

EVE and the Lady of the House were looking back over the many years they had been firm friends. They recalled momentous events on the world stage and important moments in their lives, but mostly they delighted in recalling the fashions in clothes that had come and gone.

"Ah, it's easy to come and go," Eve reflected, smiling. "The hard thing is to remain."

"That's what good friends do," the Lady of the House said.

Friday – **August 17**

WHEN eating a fruit, think of the person who planted the tree.

Vietnamese Proverb

Saturday – ***August 18***

"DO you ever wish ...?" Rachel sighed as she watched the pretty girls pass by the bench where she sat with husband Henry.

"No, I never do." Henry took her hand. "When you are in your teens your looks are down to genes or nature, but to be beautiful at our age – I couldn't manage it but I'm so glad you could!"

As Marie Stopes said, "You can take no credit for beauty at 16. But if you are beautiful at 60 it will be your own soul's doing."

Rachel has a beautiful soul and it shows. So does Henry!

Sunday – ***August 19***

EVERYONE deserves a second chance! It's easy to say, but not so easy to do if that person has hurt you. In denying them a second chance you might protect yourself from getting hurt again, but you might also be cutting yourself off from the good that person could do in future.

Two travellers and a boy were making their way through Turkey, when they came to some "badlands". The boy, Mark, turned tail and ran away. One traveller wanted to forgive his weakness, the other vowed never to, and so they fell out about it.

Later, in dire straits of his own, the man who would not forgive did forgive. He was the Apostle Paul. And the foolish boy was given the chance to go on to better things, such as writing the Gospel Of Mark.

"Now instead, you ought to forgive and comfort him, so that he will not be overwhelmed by excessive sorrow. I urge you, therefore, to reaffirm your love for him."

(Corinthians II 7-8)

Monday — ***August 20***

SO you always nursed an ambition to be an astronaut when young? Or maybe a top-of-the-bill entertainer?

Well, I don't suppose many of us will ever quite make those dizzy heights, but there's no need to feel despondent. Keep in mind these wise words of William Wordsworth:

"The best portion of a good man's life; his little nameless, unremembered acts of kindness and of love."

Goals we are all surely capable of reaching.

Tuesday — ***August 21***

WE can live perfectly well by keeping ourselves to ourselves, we might argue, choosing not to have much contact with others.

But surely we can do better than that. We can choose to set an example, give good advice, help, comfort, reassure, cheer, support and inspire. And for all of these we need contact with other people.

As Albert Einstein said: "A person only starts to live when he can live outside of himself."

Wednesday — ***August 22***

SOME people might travel the world, go on courses, or go into retreat to try to find themselves. Others, who might have been defined by their children or their work, will have moved to a time in their lives when these roles no longer apply.

Do you know what Mahatma Gandhi would say to these people? He'd say: "Get lost!"

No, he wouldn't be being nasty, he would be giving very practical advice. After all, as he said: "The best way to find yourself is to lose yourself in the service of others."

Thursday – ***August 23***

THE great industrialist Henry Ford once described enthusiasm as "the sparkle in your eyes, the swing in your gait, the grip of your hand, the irresistible surge of will and the energy to execute your ideas. Enthusiasts have fortitude. They have staying qualities. Enthusiasm is at the bottom of all progress."

The word "enthusiasm" comes from the Greek words "en theos" which mean "in God". Is it any wonder enthusiasts achieve so much?

Friday – ***August 24***

HUGH was recalling boyhood adventures by the river, especially one game where, by a series of careful leaps, he could make his way from rock to rock to the other side.

We'll come across plenty of "rocks" as we journey through life. But, as Hugh says, "I suppose it's up to us whether we make them stumbling blocks – or stepping stones!"

Saturday – ***August 25***

IF you choose to study art, exhibit at the Royal Academy, and eventually return to your homeland as Professor of Painting and Sculpture at the University of New York, then I imagine you might well feel surprised to find that your name lives on not as an artist, but as an inventor.

Yet such was the fate of Samuel Morse. It was during a sea voyage that he happened to hear a discussion of electromagnets, and that was to be the spark that led to the development of the electric telegraph, and the code that enabled a giant leap forward in the field of long-distance communication.

In later life he became well known for his donations to good causes, but his greatest gift to the world came in the form of dots and dashes.

Sunday – ***August 26***

OG MANDINO was the world's best-selling self-help author in his lifetime. His wife once recalled how this former Second World War bomber pilot used to plan his writing by sitting at his desk and staring at the blank wall in front of him, as if he was trying to fit together the pieces of a giant, invisible jigsaw.

Mandino's philosophy was Bible-based. He believed that success was no mystery and that God provided all the pieces of that jigsaw. We just have to look for them, he felt, and be prepared to fit them into our lives.

"Open my eyes that I may see wonderful things in your law." (Psalms 119:18)

Monday – ***August 27***

NICHOLAS Black Elk was a Sioux Medicine Man who saw no difficulty in combining the faith of his people with the Christianity he adopted after living in Great Britain. Perhaps feeling cut off from his familiar world in the hustle and bustle of London, he offered some advice that works equally well for those of us dealing with difficult people or situations.

"Some little root of the sacred tree still lives," he said. "Nourish it."

In other words there really is good in everyone and in every situation. It's up to us to find it and help it grow!

Tuesday – ***August 28***

IT is a sweet thing, friendship, a dear balm,
A happy and auspicious bird of calm . . .

Percy Bysshe Shelley

Homecoming

Wednesday — ***August 29***

MIKE retired recently, so when he called round to borrow a book I asked him if he was finding it easy to fill his time.

"From today onwards, yes!" he laughed. "You see, I went to my grandson's school assembly this morning. Seeing the children so eager to try new things and refusing to place any limits on their talents made me realise how many things I'd told myself I'd never be any good at. So now I'm going to use my time to try all of them."

Three cheers for such ambition. As Thomas Alva Edison said: "If we did the things we are capable of, we would astound ourselves!"

Thursday — ***August 30***

LOVE the moment. Flowers grow out of dark moments. Therefore, each moment is vital. It affects the whole. Life is a succession of such moments and to live each, is to succeed.

Corita Kent

Friday — ***August 31***

OUR friend Rebecca passed on these wise words for living well and I'd like to share them with you today:

Do all the good you can to all the folk you can as long as ever you can.

Do as the bee does with flowers – take the honey and leave the thorn.

Do good turns by stealth and tell no-one.

Do something about it – don't just wait for something to happen.

Always do what you feel is right.

September

Saturday – **September 1**

IT'S a word I have used on many occasions without really giving it much thought. It's a word we are all familiar with and most of us use daily – it's *Thanks.* We know how to use it and we know the good that comes from it, but what does it actually mean?

Well, it comes from the same root word as "think" so when we say, "I thank you," what we are really saying is, "I will think of you." So presumably, because the person has done a good thing, the thoughts will be warm ones.

It's a nice feeling to be thanked and now we know why. After all, what's better in this world than to be well thought of by others?

Sunday – **September 2**

IN the days before the world was properly explored map-makers would fill in the blank areas of their maps with phrases like, "Here there be dragons" or "Here be monsters".

Sir John Franklin, the famous maritime explorer, was said to scribble these notes out when he found them and replace them with: "Here is God". A reminder, perhaps, that there is no place unknown to Him and whatever situation we find ourselves in He is already there. "You answer us with awesome deeds of righteousness, O God our Saviour, the hope of all the ends of the earth and of the farthest seas."

(Psalms 65:5)

Monday — ***September 3***

"LOVE, honour and obey," is a phrase that's largely fallen away from the modern wedding ceremony. But did you know that "obey" and "hear" both come from the same Latin word, *audire*? All these centuries ago and usually in reference to God, to hear and to obey were, literally, one and the same thing!

Newlyweds, and even those who have been together for a long time, could do worse than promise to hear their partner. After all, hearing and taking on board what your partner is saying is surely one of the best ways to love and to honour them.

Tuesday — ***September 4***

ARE you feeling mentally and spiritually undernourished? Then here are a few words to whet your appetite:

"Worry is today's mice nibbling on tomorrow's cheese."
Anon.

"God gives all the birds their food, but he doesn't drop it into their nests."
Danish Proverb

Finally, here is one more thought to digest from the Talmud: "A quotation at the right moment is like bread to the famished"

Bon appetit!

Wednesday — ***September 5***

THE legendary jazz composer and musician, Duke Ellington, summed up the secret of his success in these simple words:

"A problem," he said, "is the perfect chance for you to do your best."

Time For Reflection

Thursday – **September 6**

GREAT things are done in the name of faith. Built in the 12th century, Kilwinning Abbey brought the town and its founders wealth and renown. But a certain thatched house standing in the shadow of the abbey would have been no less spiritual a place.

The lintel above the door, through which miners and labourers passed and under which barefoot children played, was engraved with the words, *Sine Te Domine Cuncta Nil*, or, "Without Thee, Lord, it's all for nothing".

A reminder, surely, that faith does its greatest work not in grand buildings, but in the home!

Friday – **September 7**

IN parts of Mexico there are hot and cold springs beside each other. Local people used to take advantage of this by boiling their washing in one spring and rinsing it in the other. A real example of bountiful nature, you might think.

But according to a tour guide some people still complained they had to supply their own soap . . .

Mother Nature might not do our washing for us, but this world is still a wonderful gift! So, let's not complain if we occasionally have to contribute some "soap" to the mix.

Saturday – **September 8**

SUSANNE likes to collect proverbs and other wise sayings and keeps a scrapbook with her favourites to share with friends and family and to dip into.

These include this centuries'-old proverb: "Tell me and I'll forget; show me and I may remember; teach me and I'll learn."

Sunday – **September 9**

WE thank you for the harvest, Lord,
The bounty of your hand,
For every season of the year
Which touches all the land.
For fruit and flowers, trees and plants,
The miracle of seeds,
For food and comfort through the months
Providing for our needs.

We thank you for the love we share,
The harvest of the heart,
For all the precious gifts of life
Your hope and joy impart.
We pray for those less fortunate
Who suffer every day,
Be with them on their journey, Lord,
And help them find the way.

And now, once more, we thank you, Lord,
For blessings great and small,
But most of all, your endless love,
The greatest gift of all.

Iris Hesselden

Monday – **September 10**

DO you ever wish for a life with no problems? Our friend John must have been thinking along those lines when he complained to me about his "work" load. At the time there was a dispute between two friends which he was fairly sure he could help with, and he still had to round up lots more volunteers to help with a good cause.

That's when John quoted George Bernard Shaw: "If there were nothing wrong in the world," he said, "there wouldn't be anything for us to do."

Tuesday — ***September 11***

OUR friend Pamela had been looking after her grandson. "You know, there's nothing quite like having a small child around," she said with a smile.

"It certainly reminds us just how full of wonders the world really is. Whether it's a daisy growing in a field, or catching sight of a butterfly on a bush, young Jack finds it all astonishing and absorbing. And, you know, because I'm with him, so do I."

Her comments made me think of these words from the writer Ray Bradbury who exuberantly observed: "Stuff your eyes with wonder . . . See the world. It's more fantastic than any dream made or paid for in factories."

Wednesday — ***September 12***

THERE are so many amazing things to discover as we go through life and with each new day we are given the opportunity to become a little wiser. Here are a few points to ponder:

Frame mishaps with these words: In five years, will this matter?
Over-prepare, then go with the flow.
Don't take yourself so seriously. No one else does.

Thursday — ***September 13***

LAST year when our friend Rose faced a number of challenges, a card of encouragement arrived in the post. In it the Lady of the House had written these words: *A little faith will bring your soul to heaven, but a lot of faith will bring heaven to your soul.*

Those words still strengthen her even now when the storm clouds of life have passed.

Friday – **September 14**

I HEARD the radio in the background when I called round to see our friend Ian. "I've just been listening to a programme about Willie Nelson," he told me.

"I already knew quite a bit about him – that he's long been a remarkable singer and songwriter, that he's had plenty of ups and downs in his career, and that he's never believed in following convention, but I hadn't realised quite how much wisdom he'd picked up along the way.

"I particularly liked his comment, 'I believe that all life is connected, and that there is beauty and value in all things. I believe that truth is found in our own heart. The trick is to shut up and listen'."

Yes, definitely something to sing about!

Saturday – **September 15**

WE'RE often told beware of pride –
It comes before a fall,
Yet I can think of many times
It's not so bad at all:
For everyone should take some pride
In being kind and good,
Take rightful pride in all your skills,
And use them as you should.
And, yes, take pride in having friends,
They're gifts of utmost worth,
Take pride in every time you try
To beautify this earth.
So don't be shy or hide away,
Make sure your talents shine
And you will find a little pride
Is absolutely fine!

Margaret Ingall

Sunday – **September 16**

"OH, I am burdened this morning!" Robert Chapman, the 19th-century preacher, had given up a comfortable lifestyle for a workman's house in the shadow of a tannery giving out a strong smell. His pantry was empty more often than not and he had plenty to complain about.

"Oh, yes," he continued that day. "I am burdened with an over-abundance of blessings for which I can never find enough time or words to express my gratitude."

Like most of us Chapman had reason to complain – but he also knew he had greater reason to smile. As Genesis 49:26 says: "Your Father's blessings are greater than the blessings of the ancient mountains, than the bounty of the age-old hills."

Monday – **September 17**

OUR old friend Mary told us that her mother's wise sayings included these memorable words, ones well worth passing on:

No matter how you feel, get up, dress up and
show up.
Life isn't tied with a bow, but it's still a gift.
When in doubt, just take the next small step.
All that truly matters in the end is that you loved.

Tuesday – **September 18**

THE Lady of the House caught sight of this saying on the sign outside a church: *The task ahead of us is never as great as the power behind us.*

How true!

Wednesday – **September 19**

THERE'S no doubt about it – however much we may plan for and look forward to changes of circumstance in our lives, few of us can embrace the prospect without any misgivings.

Maxine, for example, was thrilled to find that she was expecting a baby, but she was also just a little nervous as to how she and her husband would be affected by such a huge change to their way of living. Happily, she had a friend who had herself recently become a mother, and who was able to pass on this quote from Vincent Van Gogh:

"I think that I see something deeper, more infinite, more eternal than the ocean in the expression of the eyes of a little baby when it wakes in the morning and coos or laughs because it sees the sun shining on the cradle."

Sometimes a few words of encouragement can do far more good than we ever realise.

Thursday – **September 20**

TWO neighbours, James and Isabel, were going round to our old friend Mary for coffee one morning. When they arrived James mentioned – with a smile – that they would have been there sooner if his beloved hadn't felt the need to spend so much time in front of the mirror. At that point Isabel pointed out that, in fact, she had had to wait for James to move aside before she could get near the mirror.

"Well, I find the world's like a mirror," Mary said. "If I go out wearing a dour expression, then I generally find the world looks a little duller. But if I leave the house with a smile, then the world reflects my happiness and adds some of its own."

Now, how's your reflection looking today?

Friday – **September 21**

I HADN'T intended to spend the afternoon indoors, but the downpour was so heavy that my plans for a walk were completely washed away. However, an hour among my books did provide some rather consoling thoughts:

"Rain! Whose soft architectural hands have power to cut stones and chisel to shapes of grandeur the very mountains."

Henry Ward Beecher

"Water is the most expressive element in nature. It responds to every mood from tranquillity to turbulence."

Walter J. Phillips

"How beautiful is the rain! After the dust and the heat, in the broad and fiery street, In the narrow lane, How beautiful is the rain!" Henry Wadsworth Longfellow

So my afternoon did have a silver lining, after all!

Saturday – **September 22**

MANY hundreds of years ago a group of Christians became hermits in the Sinai desert in imitation of their Master who spent 40 days and nights in the wilderness. They lived solitary lives in caves existing on what little they could forage and in complete silence. Their aim was to become closer to God.

One day a traveller came across one of these hermits, who welcomed him warmly to his cave, shared his meal and talked and prayed with him. Later, as he was on the point of leaving the visitor said, "Forgive me, for I have made you break your rule."

The hermit answered, "My rule is to receive you with hospitality and send you away in peace."

From The Orchard

Sunday – **September 23**

NINE-year-old Katie had invited her friend, Becky, along to church. Becky then attended for a couple of weeks when the clergyman, who had been ill, came back to deliver his first sermon in many months.

After saying how good it felt to be back, he said: "And how nice it is to see a new face. What's your name?"

Becky looked this way and that to see who he was talking to. Surely he couldn't be addressing her?

In this busy world we might feel like we are lost in the crowd, but when God looks down, He doesn't see the multitude. He sees you and He's talking to you.

"She gave this name to the Lord who spoke to her: 'You are the God who sees me,' for she said, 'I have now seen the one who sees me'."

(Genesis 16:13)

Monday – **September 24**

"I SOMETIMES wonder," Grant puffed, as he clambered his way up the hill, "just why we humans are so fond of a good view. Perhaps it's because we like to see what lies ahead of us."

We all love the feeling of knowing in advance what we're about to face – and yet so often in life we can find ourselves deep in a valley, unsure which path can lead us out of it.

If you happen to be in that valley now, take courage. Sooner or later and even if it does take some effort, you will find yourself on the brow of that hill with the world spread out before you. Enjoy that moment – like Grant, you'll have earned it!

Tuesday — **September 25**

HERE are some of Mother Teresa's thoughts on love to share today:

Love is a fruit in season at all times, and within reach of every hand.

Do not think that love, in order to be genuine, has to be extraordinary. What we need is to love without getting tired.

Good works are links that form a chain of love.

Spread love everywhere you go. Let no one ever come to you without leaving happier.

Wednesday — **September 26**

THE lines of power
That change my life
Are Heaven's dower.
For my belief.

His chandelier
Is shining proof,
His lantern's fire
Is light enough.

Though every hour,
All through my life,
Old doubts devour,
New burden's bluff.

My lines of power
Hum with relief,
Give lie the fear,
Godspeed the grief.

John Ellis

Thursday – **September 27**

A FRIEND shared with me this great advice from the Anthony Robbins Organisation. Mr Robbins believes that your life will be enriched if you apply principles such as these:

Give people more than they expect and do it cheerfully. When you say, "I'm sorry," look the person in the eye. Love deeply and passionately. You might get hurt, but it's the only way to live completely. Talk slowly, but think quickly.

Remember that great love and great achievements involve great risk. When you lose, don't lose the lesson. Don't let a little dispute injure a great friendship. When you've realised you've made a mistake, take immediate steps to correct it. Smile when picking up the phone; the caller will hear it in your voice.

Friday – **September 28**

CELIA and Debbie had been discussing their favourite kind of television programmes. Though they varied in their tastes, there was one sort on which they were both agreed: "feel-good" documentaries came top of the list.

"There's nothing quite as satisfying as watching real people achieving their goals, or helping others to realise their dreams," Celia said. "Not only do they remind us that life isn't all doom and gloom, they really do make us 'feel good' about the whole human race."

And that's the sort of fresh attitude to life which never becomes boring. As author Robert A. Heinlein said: "One of the sanest, surest, and most generous joys of life comes from being happy over the good fortune of others."

Saturday – **September 29**

FOR many years we two have walked together
Along the steep and bumpy path of life,
Carving our initials by the wayside
With childish chalk, and youth's impatient knife.
Using up the pristine hopes of springtime,
The blazing heat and strength of summer's sun,
Always there, the one to help the other
When dragons must be slain, and battles won.
Now, as we pick the mellow fruits of autumn,
To lay in stocks, against the winter's chill,
I watch you glance into a full-length mirror
To see if Time has used you good or ill.
But you need never, ever fear the blighting
Of all that's fair, whatever fate may send.
For there's a shining brightness deep within you,
Which warms my heart. You're beautiful, my friend.

Tricia Sturgeon.

Sunday – **September 30**

ONE day, Geoff was remembering his Sunday school days. "We nearly always finished with a rousing rendition of 'God Be With You Till We Meet Again'," he said. "I must admit in those days I enjoyed it simply because it meant it was nearly time to go home. Yet those words have stayed with me throughout my life, and I've often been comforted by the verse:

God be with you till we meet again,
When life's perils thick confound you,
Put His arms unfailing round you,
God be with you till we meet again."

It was Jeremiah Eames Rankin who wrote those words, and I suspect they have cheered and encouraged many people throughout the years.

October

Monday – **October 1**

SALLY had been telling me about her great-aunt Alice, who has a great fondness for quoting proverbs. "Her favourite is 'Look before you leap'," she said. "After all, I suppose it's quite a sensible piece of advice."

"But you have a better one?" I asked, prompted by the twinkle in her eye.

"I do indeed," she laughed. "Although it's not quite as pithy, I prefer this thought from Marie Beyon Ray, who said: 'Begin doing what you want to do now. We have only this moment, sparkling like a star in our hand – and melting like a snowflake'."

Well, looking before you leap might be the safer option, but oh – all those snowflakes we'd never get to see!

Tuesday – **October 2**

AS I watched the bank of trees sway in the autumn winds my attention was drawn to some of the newer saplings. How, I wondered, would they cope when the rougher winter winds arrived?

After a moment's thought I walked on, reassured. Just as in our lives we tend to see "storms" as negative things, in reality they are what make us – and trees – stronger. The Welsh poet, George Herbert, had it right when he wrote, "Storms make oaks take deeper root."

My friends the saplings would be fine!

Wednesday — **October 3**

WHEN our old friend Mary woke up one morning the sun was shining brightly and as she opened a window, she could smell the scent of flowers wafting towards her. In fact, she said later, it was such a glorious morning that she couldn't help but be grateful and rejoice in its beauty.

Nathaniel Hawthorne said: "Our creator would never have made such lovely days and have given us the deep hearts to enjoy them, above and beyond all thought, unless we were meant to be immortal."

Regardless of circumstances, or what the weather may be or what yesterday held, give thanks for the beauty before you.

Thursday — **October 4**

ARISTOTLE, the Greek philosopher, had these wise words to say about the value of friendship:

Without friends no-one would choose to live, though he had all other goods.

Friday — **October 5**

AS irrigators lead water where they want, as archers make their arrows straight, as carpenters carve wood, the wise shape their minds. So says Buddha.

"I must admit," the Lady of the House said, "that when I first read those words, I wasn't sure what to make of them. But then the idea of those craftsmen carefully using their skills to the very best of their abilities made me think. For yes, it's in just those ways that we should be shaping our best and finest tools — our intellect and mind.

"So in future I'll do my best to lead my thoughts away from unhelpful feelings, keep it sharp with new challenges and bright with positive thinking."

I think we could *all* try, don't you?

Saturday – **October 6**

THE 19th-century artist and cartoonist Thomas Nast had an interesting party trick. He would place a long canvas on an easel and paint a landscape on it. Then, in a moment of seeming madness he would "ruin" it all with broad strokes of dark colour.

While his audience looked on shocked and puzzled, Nast's assistants would tilt the painting up on its end to show it was actually a completely unexpected picture, perhaps a woodland scene or a tumbling waterfall.

Life can do to us what Nast did to his picture. The things we hope for might never come to pass, but if we adjust our point of view there might be a new, surprisingly beautiful future there!

Sunday – **October 7**

IT'S sad but true that even in the closest of relationships, there can be occasions when things don't run smoothly. Sometimes this can simply be due to time spent apart from each other, but even when together we may feel separated by feelings of having been misunderstood or taken for granted.

Happily, with goodwill on both sides, most problems can usually be smoothed out, but meanwhile let us try never to forget that the most important relationship of all is indestructible:

"Neither death, nor life, nor angels, nor principalities, nor powers, nor things present, nor things to come, nor height, nor depth, nor any other creatures, shall be able to separate us from the love of God, which is in Christ Jesus our Lord."

(Romans 8:38)

Green And Gold

Monday — **October 8**

HERE are 10 Native American Commandments, wise words to keep in mind at any time.

Treat Mother Earth and all who dwell thereon
with respect.
Remain close to the Great Spirit.
Show great respect for your fellow beings.
Work together for the benefit of all mankind.
Give assistance and kindness wherever needed.
Do what you know is right.
Look after the wellbeing of mind and body.
Dedicate a share of your efforts to the greater good.
Be truthful and honest at all times.
Take full responsibility for your actions.

Tuesday — **October 9**

IT'S been an up-and-down sort of year for Scott. First came difficult times at work and then a broken ankle but also the excitement and delight of becoming a grandfather.

"Every incident," he told me, "whether good or bad, has been helped and improved by the knowledge that friends have cared what happened to me."

It's good to remember that life is made up of such small, though vital, human connections.

John Donne put it far more beautifully: "No man is an island entire of itself; every man is a piece of the continent, a part of the main."

Wednesday — **October 10**

HERE are some words worth keeping in mind as we go through every day of the year: *We are not what we think we are, but what we think, we are.*

Thursday – **October 11**

"YOU know, I wasn't looking forward to this afternoon," our friend John admitted. "I knew I needed to sweep up the fallen leaves, and it's always a job that makes me feel gloomy about the end of summer. But I hadn't long made a start when my neighbour's young son came round to lend a hand.

"He *did* help me sweep them all up eventually, but not before he'd had great fun jumping into the drift and kicking them up into the air. Watching him get such pleasure from them taught me the wisdom of taking time to enjoy the moment, rather than dwelling on the past or future."

So, try not to let *your* happy moments flutter by unappreciated!

Friday – **October 12**

WHAT can we do when news we'd rather not hear comes our way? Well, first of all, we should try to remember that there has been unexpected news before.

With courage and determination we can turn bad news into better news – and we can do so again and again! It all depends how we face up to the challenges of life.

Saturday – **October 13**

A FRIEND once sent the Lady of the House a card with this little verse, one which she has always cherished. May it bring a blessing to your day:

Look back and thank God.
Look forward and trust God.
Look around and serve God.
Look within and find God.

Sunday – **October 14**

GUILLEMOTS spend most of their lives at sea. The birds come to land just to lay their eggs and they only do this on the steepest cliffs. As space is very much at a premium, rows and rows of identical eggs are laid side by side on narrow, rocky outcrops – identical to everyone that is, but the mothers.

Ornithologists found that if they moved an egg from one part of a ledge to another, the mother bird could tell the difference and would seek it out, returning her egg to its original place.

We might sometimes feel unnoticed, or lost in the crowd around us, but just as the guillemot knows her eggs from all the scores of others, so God the Father can always find His children.

"Nevertheless, God's solid foundation stands firm, sealed with the inscription, 'The Lord knows those who are his'."
(Timothy 2:19)

Monday – **October 15**

HER background was one of impoverishment and abandonment. She toured for years with a penniless drama company before getting her break on Broadway and moving to California. Mary Pickford would eventually make the transition from being "The Girl With The Curls," to "The Woman Who Made Hollywood".

The secret of her success isn't hard to find. "If you have made mistakes," she said, "there is always another chance for you, for this thing we call failure is not the falling down, but the staying down."

When life seems hard, remember The Girl With The Curls. Take that other chance.

Tuesday – **October 16**

ERNEST Shackleton's 1914 Antarctic expedition turned into a heroic rescue operation. Later he was asked what the worst moment had been for him and he described waking in the middle of the night in a storm-lashed tent.

His men were starving and that's when he caught sight of a trusted companion reach out and take a sleeping man's food bag. That was the worst moment.

The other man surreptitiously put the last of his own food in the bag and tucked it back into the sleeping man's kit. "I dare not tell you his name," Shackleton said, "for I feel his act was a secret between him and God."

We should all have secrets like that!

Wednesday – **October 17**

A KEEN botanist was telling me about a type of lily that grows in the desert. Somehow it survives the lack of water, sand storms and scorching heat.

"Not only that," he said, "but the worse the winter the bigger and better the blooms next summer. It's as if it was sending out a challenge to the elements to do their worst."

I think these lilies have a message for all of us, don't you?

Thursday – **October 18**

OUR friend Carole recalls that a tradesman who did work at her childhood home used to quote these words: "Measure twice before you saw once."

In other words, think carefully before you act – a golden rule for all of us, whatever we are doing.

Friday – **October 19**

HAVE you heard of Ralston Young? He wasn't apparently anyone special. In fact, hundreds of people walked past him every day. Ralston was a porter at New York's Central Station and in those crowds of travellers he saw the opportunity to do good every day.

"You know," he would say, "everybody going through Central Station isn't going on honeymoon or to a party. Many are going to funerals, the hospital or even prison." He would get to know the people whose bags he carried and minister the best he could to those in need.

One bag at a time, one weary traveller after another, this man helped thousands of people.

Saturday – **October 20**

PEACE and faith and love and hope,
Four candles burning low,
Yet side by side they lit the night
And gave a warming glow.
But anger soon diminished peace
As faith gave in to doubt,
And love, abandoned, faded too,
And soon all three went out.

But hope still kept her flame alight
A joy for all to see,
And growing stronger through the dark,
She soon relit all three!
When peace and faith and love grow dim
And struggle to survive,
Hold fast to hope through doubt and fear
And keep the flame alive.

Iris Hesselden

Sunday – **October 21**

AGATE is a semi-precious stone that's often used to make all kinds of jewellery. No two are the same and the patterns, made from volcanic processes, can be wonderfully varied. But most of us would walk past agate on a pebble beach!

Then an expert might come by. He would pick out the stone he wants from all the others, scrub it and polish it before mounting it in precious metal and showing the world its inner beauty.

In the same way, our Father can pick out his children in any crowd and He has something quite different in mind for each of us. He doesn't promise an easy journey as we go through life, but he does promise us the finished product will be worth the effort.

"For our light and momentary troubles are achieving for us an eternal glory that far outweighs them all."

(Corinthians II 4:17)

Monday – **October 22**

FOR the past year our friend Don has been training to run a marathon. There are certainly times when the prospect intimidates him, he admits, and then he begins to wonder why he took on such a formidable challenge. He sometimes worries about how long it will take to complete the training and how his final race time will compare to that of more seasoned runners.

One day he came across this quote on my desk and he has taken its words to heart: "Yesterday I dared to struggle. Today I dare to win."

Powerful words to live – and run – by!

Tuesday – **October 23**

"MY childhood ambition was to be a teacher," Olive said, "but somehow it never quite happened. So now I just help out at the children's drama group instead."

Olive's use of the word "just" did not do her justice. Her efforts have inspired so many local youngsters over the years, teaching them confidence and commitment, helping them to explore and discover their own talents.

There are many people like Olive in this world, and their generosity brings to mind the words of Benjamin Disraeli: "The greatest good you can do for another is not just share your riches, but reveal to them their own."

Now, that's the kind of giving that lasts for ever!

Wednesday – **October 24**

DURING a sermon, Claire's clergyman spoke about how our faith may be tested. There is nothing wrong with having doubts during these times, he said – when we embrace doubt and allow ourselves to experience it, our faith becomes stronger.

He quoted Thomas Merton, who said, "Say to the darkness I am not afraid."

Good advice in uncertain times.

Thursday – **October 25**

CONSIDER these eloquent words which celebrate our age and accomplishments:

"The years teach much which the days never knew."
Ralph Waldo Emerson

"The spiritual eyesight improves as the physical eyesight declines."
Plato

The Turning

Friday – **October 26**

I WONDER if you know the story of Luther Burbank, the American plant wizard? He was born in Massachusetts in 1849 and brought up on a farm.

Luther went on to establish both a nursery garden and experimental farms in Santa Rosa, California, where he pursued his interest in botany and horticulture. Many beautiful garden plants grown today were patiently bred or carefully improved by Luther Burbank through selection and crossing of one plant with another; this includes the lily family. He also developed a spineless cactus, which was useful for cattle feed, and the Russet Burbank potato.

During his 55 years of plant breeding, Luther developed more than 800 new and improved varieties and became world famous for his useful work. He said: "I love humanity which has been a constant delight to me . . . and I love flowers, trees, animals and all the works of nature as they pass before us in time and space."

Saturday – **October 27**

ONE evening our young friend Hannah invited some of her friends round to share a meal and, as they sat down to eat, recited this grace:

As we raise our knives and forks,
As we pop the champagne corks,
Lord, let us remember if we may,
Those who will not eat today.

Four simple lines that made everyone present think about the food in front of them and where it had all come from. Perhaps we might like to keep these words in mind, too, when we next sit down to eat.

Sunday – ***October 28***

AFTER a lengthy walk in the country, Frank decided to reward his collie, Bracken, with some special canine treats. He placed each little biscuit on his knee while Bracken sat to attention.

When Frank said, "Take it!" Bracken snapped up his reward. Between commands, Bracken never looked at the treat. He was completely focused on his master.

Sometimes we pay too much attention to the treats of this life. We become wrapped up in the pursuit of material gain with the corresponding fears and insecurities. For certainty and peace of mind we could learn a lesson from Bracken and look beyond the immediate reward, focusing instead on the One from whom everything ultimately comes.

"O Sovereign Lord, you are God! Your words are trustworthy and you have promised these good things to your servant."

(Samuel II 7:28)

Monday – ***October 29***

ANDREW and Heather were on their way home from an enjoyable outing to local seaside illuminations, so perhaps it's not surprising that talk turned to the subject of street-lighting, and how easy it is to take for granted all inventions.

Heather came up with this quotation from Felix Adler: "The hero is the one who kindles a great light in the world, who sets up blazing torches in the dark streets of life for men to see by. The saint is the man who walks through the dark paths of the world, himself a light."

I don't suppose many of us could claim to be either hero or saint, but we can certainly see the light and be grateful for both!

Tuesday — **October 30**

IT'S as simple as breathing! I'd almost forgotten that exasperated catchphrase from my schooldays until I read about John Scott Haldane. Born in 1860 into an old and illustrious Scottish family, it would have been easy for him to coast through life but instead he chose to study science, researching the influence of air quality on human health, aimed at helping the poorest of the population.

He walked city slums, analysing the adverse effect of factory fumes, and raising awareness of the dangerous levels of carbon dioxide. He visited coal mines to examine – and find out how to prevent – the poisonous gasses which were claiming the lives of so many of the workers. He even frequently used himself as a guinea-pig in a series of risky experiments.

John Scott Haldane, I'm happy to say, did survive into old age – and what's more, his work allowed a great many others to do so as well.

Wednesday — **October 31**

THE guest organist at the cathedral entertained his listeners with a mix of melodies from Handel to The Beatles. After each tune he turned and acknowledged the applause. When he finished his set, he stood for the ovation and gave the audience a round of applause in return, then he turned and directed the applause to the organ.

After all, he didn't make the mighty instrument and without it his efforts would have been to no avail.

Our lives are like that. We get to use them, but we didn't make them – they are gifts. What we can do is make some beautiful music with them, and every so often we might take the time to applaud the Great Composer.

November

Thursday – ***November 1***

A READER sent me a postcard from the Grace Darling Museum in Northumberland. As I'm sure many are aware, Grace was the daughter of the Longstone lighthouse keeper, who in 1848, together with her father, rowed out through ferocious seas and gales in the hope of rescuing several shipwrecked passengers.

It's a stirring tale, and one which brings to mind the words of Ambrose Redmoon: "Courage is not the absence of fear, but rather the judgment that something else is more important than fear."

I suspect that when Grace Darling made her decision to risk her life in the hope of saving others, she not only achieved her aim but gave courage and inspiration to more people than she could ever have imagined.

Friday – ***November 2***

HARRY was waiting for a bus on a wooded stretch of road when a friend stopped for a chat. He pointed to the bare branches and said that it was a shame all the green was gone.

However, Harry pointed beyond the branches to the clear sky and said, "The green may be gone – but that just lets us see more blue."

Harry is forever the optimist. Even when he's "blue", it's a good thing!

Saturday – **November 3**

A MAN was busy in his garden when a stranger happened to pass by.

"Have you lived here long?" he asked.

"I have lived here all my life – 100 years," he replied.

"Indeed? But I see you are planting fruit trees," said the stranger.

The man nodded.

"But surely you will not be here to gather the fruit from these saplings?" enquired the stranger, puzzled.

"Well," replied the elderly man, "when I came into this world I found many good things awaiting me, so I would like to leave good things waiting for others in turn."

Sunday – **November 4**

WHEN Rhonda and Patrick became parents some years ago they began to understand the truth in these words: "It takes a village to raise a child." Their entire neighbourhood took a deep interest in young Lila, who was born with spina bifida.

Throughout the years neighbours brought meals to the family, helped with chores, and offered babysitting and even help with cleaning. Rhonda and Patrick found that sharing the challenges of looking after Lila with their neighbours created lasting bonds.

Today Lila is a cheerful young woman who has countless "aunts" and "uncles" and knows she is loved; most are customers at the shop where she works.

"Be devoted to one another in brotherly love, Honour one another above yourselves . . . Share with God's people who are in need. Practise hospitality." (Romans 12:10,13)

Monday – **November 5**

OUR old friend Mary's bird feeder is a clear plastic tube with holes in the sides and little wooden perches under each hole. Well, one day, it seems, a woodpecker landed on a perch.

Oblivious to the holes, where it could have had seeds galore, the stubborn creature started pecking at the plastic. It hopped from perch to perch trying the same technique and achieving the same result. It took a little finch to flutter down and show the woodpecker how to get its breakfast.

"The question we might ask," Mary suggested, "is are we the kind of people who go full steam, banging our heads against a problem? Or are we the ones who gently show how it's done?"

Tuesday – **November 6**

THERE'S nothing on this earth to be prized more than true friendship.

Saint Thomas Aquinas

Wednesday – **November 7**

PHILIP, Lord Wharton, died in 1696 aged over eighty and is still remembered and referred to as "the good Lord Wharton".

In his will he left money to be used each year for the purchase and distribution of Bibles and other books for young people.

In his youth he was reputed to be handsome and he enjoyed dancing. More than three centuries later Lord Wharton's Charity still exists, and I think his dancing Lordship would have been pleased to know that his legacy is still spreading the message of Jesus, who is often called the Lord of the Dance.

Morlich Magnificence

Thursday – **November 8**

IN the space of a few days the Lady of the House met Caitlin who was about to start nursery school, Jim who had just had a story published in a well-known magazine and Emily who was about to start voluntary work in her community.

Very different people, you might think, but they shared the same air of excitement. Somehow, it reminded her of Don Quixote setting out on a brand new adventure! Then she remembered it was Miguel Cervantes who wrote: "Love not what you are – but what you may become."

Being content is a fine thing, but if we might still become better – well, there's always room for a new adventure!

Friday – **November 9**

HERE are some wise words passed on to the Lady of the House which I'd like to share with you today:

"Life does not require us to be the biggest or the best. It only asks that we try."

Saturday – **November 10**

ANN was telling me about her life spent in the Salvation Army. When she joined, 70 years ago, things were fairly strict, with the Salvation Army sharing many of the ranks and terms of the regular army.

Now, in the regular army the term AWOL is short for "absent without leave" as we all know, but back then the young recruits to the Salvation Army used the term differently. If they weren't with their colleagues actively spreading the good word, they were encouraged to be AWOL, or, "Active In Works Of Love."

I think I prefer Ann's version of these words, don't you?

Sunday – ***November 11***

THE Hollywood director Cecil B. DeMille was well known for his lavish Biblical epics like "King Of Kings" and "The Ten Commandments", but one of his most profoundly spiritual experiences can be described as a much lower budget affair.

Canoeing with friends one day, he saw water beetles swimming beneath the surface of the lake. One of the beetles climbed on to his canoe and died. After a while in the hot sun the creature's shell dried and cracked. And then a dragonfly emerged!

DeMille watched the shimmering creature buzz the surface of the water, but he knew the beetles beneath the water would never begin to understand this new and more glorious version of their creation.

"Would the creator of the universe do that for a water beetle," DeMille asked, "and do less for a human?"

"I consider that our present sufferings are not worth comparing with the glory that will be revealed in us."

(Romans 8:18)

Monday – ***November 12***

I'VE been reading a book about explorers, and I was intrigued to find that many of them had learned just as much about human nature as the places they visited all over the world.

"It's not the mountain we conquer but ourselves," said Edmund Hillary, the first climber to reach the top of Mount Everest.

"There can be no happiness if the things we believe in are different from the things we do," commented Freya Stark, adventurer and explorer.

Now these really are discoveries worth making.

Tuesday — **November 13**

THERE was once a man who had many sons who were always disagreeing about everything.

Then one day, the father collected a bundle of sticks and asked his sons to break the bundle. To no avail. They were strong but still they could not bend or snap the sticks which were so firmly tied together.

At last the father untied the bundle and his sons could easily snap the small twigs one by one.

"Now," said the father. "Do you all see what the power of unity can do? Apart you are easily broken and divided you fall. But bound together by loyalty and love you are so strong that no misfortune can ever tear you apart."

Wednesday — **November 14**

CICERO, the Roman philosopher, statesman and orator, is the source of today's thought:

"Friendship adds a brighter radiance to prosperity, and lightens the burden of adversity by dividing and sharing it."

Thursday — **November 15**

IN a novel by the Scottish writer Jane Duncan, one of her characters is complimented on having a good memory.

"Yes, and I have got a lot of good things to remember," is the reply.

That is a sound attitude to adopt, surely, for to have a memory which constantly focuses on less than pleasant events will do nothing to enrich the pleasures of everyday living.

Friday – ***November 16***

IN spite of all the ups and downs of everyday life, it is worthwhile keeping in mind the many little pleasures which help to oil the wheels when life has not been as smooth running as you would like.

I am thinking of such simple but priceless pleasures as savouring a golden-hued evening as the sun slowly sinks below the horizon reflecting a brilliant sunset; the refreshing qualities of a surprise cup of tea shared with a friend; receiving a cheerful letter from an old neighbour; sharing a joke with the youngest member of the family . . .

Such are the lighter moments in life which help to make up for the inevitable disappointments and anxieties we all encounter along the way.

Saturday – ***November 17***

HOPE is like a bird that senses the dawn and carefully starts to sing while it is still dark.

Anon

Sunday – ***November 18***

IMAGINE a couple of the less complicated wonders of creation.

Salt. It's made of sodium and chlorine. Either component, taken individually, is toxic, but combined they are one of life's essentials.

Water. It's made of hydrogen, which tends to explode, and oxygen, which helps things burn, yet when combined they'll put out a fire.

And these are two of His simpler works! Is it any wonder that God rested on the seventh day? "God saw all that he had made, and it was very good."

(Genesis 1:31)

Let's Go For
A Walk!

Monday – ***November 19***

JEAN and her four colleagues work as a close team. As a small charitable foundation that provides resources for the less well off, they rely on grants and donations and try hard to be resourceful.

Sometimes the wait for funds can be very long indeed and during those times they work together even more closely.

For example, when their sole fundraiser had to leave suddenly, Jean stepped in to fill the vacancy. She spent two days a week canvassing in addition to all her office responsibilities; her colleagues made sure she didn't get too far behind by lending her a helping hand – several in fact!

Jean and her colleagues are dedicated to serving those who need help. As the saying goes: "A successful team beats with one heart."

Tuesday – ***November 20***

"HAVE you ever watched the judges at a bagpipe competition, Francis?" our friend John asked me.

"Well, no," I replied, slightly puzzled. "Usually I'm watching the pipers."

John went on to explain that some judges listened with their hands over their ears. It wasn't that they hated bagpipe music, but by covering their ears they shut out the sound the pipes produce, allowing them to focus on the higher pitched melody.

Modern life throws up a lot of loud noise and sometimes we forget that people and nature can be well worth listening to. If you think about it for a moment, those bagpipe judges might have an idea worth imitating. Let's learn to shut out the low-level drone so that we can concentrate on the higher, more beautiful melody.

Wednesday – **November 21**

WE'VE travelled through the year together
As the weeks have slipped away,
Sharing friendship, joy and laughter,
Seeking beauty every day.
Through the green of spring and summer,
Through the autumn, red and gold,
Cherishing the precious moments,
Making memories to hold.

As we travel through the winter
May our way be smooth and bright,
And a guiding star be near us
Leading on with love and light.
May our homes have warmth and comfort
When the days are dark and drear,
And the gifts of hope and friendship
Take us safely through next year.

Iris Hesselden.

Thursday – **November 22**

ALICE Freeman Palmer was the first woman president of a major American college and also a champion of the disadvantaged. Her husband, George, often complained that she spent too much time helping the needy. Instead he thought she should be writing "worthy" books so that future generations would remember her work.

Alice Palmer died in 1902 aged 47, and it's for her charitable efforts rather than any scholarly tomes she is still remembered. Her reply to her husband's concerns might explain why.

"If you put yourself into people," she said, "they touch other people, these in turn touch others still, and so you go on working – forever."

Friday – ***November 23***

A ROBIN lived in one of our Canadian friend Freda's maple trees and the mother bird was teaching her baby to fly. One day, Freda watched the two of them for a long time. The youngster was clearly afraid and sat on the edge of the nearby porch for almost 20 minutes, hardly moving.

Its mother hopped over to him and then flew away repeatedly, encouraging him to follow. Finally the youngster made a clumsy attempt and fluttered awkwardly a little way down into the unknown. But Mother would not give up and she coaxed him out across the lawn where they tried to fly together again and again.

Freda was moved at such a tender display of maternal devotion. We need not look very far to find God's little miracles.

Saturday – ***November 24***

MANDY'S work involves making a lot of business calls on the telephone. Her predecessor left a list of suggestions for making effective calls which Mandy included in her new routine:

Call a regular client at the same time each day. Honour that time.

Establish your objective before you pick up the receiver.

Develop a pleasing voice, which comes from a pleasant attitude.

Sit up straight. This call is important.

You won't always get the decision maker, so try to make the decision maker's assistant your friend.

"Is it just me," Mandy said thoughtfully, "or do those sound like fine suggestions for prayer as well?"

I'd say so.

Sunday – **November 25**

THE builders of the new Wembley Stadium boast that every seat points towards the centre and there are no obstructed views. But for how much of each football match will the football fans be looking at the centre?

Not long, probably, as the action constantly moves around the pitch. Sometimes, if they're talking to friends, the fans might not even be looking at the pitch.

Our lives are a bit like Wembley, with the centre of the universe, spiritually speaking, right in front of us and there are no obstructed views. We only have to ignore the distractions long enough to look.

"Look to the Lord and his strength; seek his face always."
(Psalms 105:4)

Monday – **November 26**

IF, when young, you'd studied hard and spent most of your precious spare time working to find a place at university, just think how devastating it would feel to be forced to drop out early because of poor eyesight. That was exactly what happened to Ohio-born Charles Francis Kettering in the late 1800s.

It would be understandable if such a blow had left him feeling bitter, but this man eventually went on to carve out a remarkable career as an engineer and inventor, developing ideas ranging from harnessing solar energy to incubators for premature babies.

"You can't have a better tomorrow if you are thinking about yesterday all the time," he once said.

What wonderful tomorrows we could share if we all learned from his wisdom.

Tuesday – **November 27**

INSPIRING and uplifting thoughts
Bring beauty to the mind,
By dwelling on the positive
What's joyful, happy, kind.
Courage and enthusiasm
Cheerfulness and grace,
Radiating from within
All show upon the face.

Reflecting on the beautiful
What's pure and good and true,
Embracing all the world of wonder
That's surrounding you.
Hope, contentment, peace and love
Your thoughts can soar on wings –
So let the life within your mind
Be filled with lovely things.

Kathleen Gillum

Wednesday – **November 28**

TERRY walks daily on a route near his home that was once a railway line. At one point it passes near a huge gravel pit. There are No Trespassing signs posted on trees, warning hikers and cyclists of danger and the noise of trucks and excavators nearby seems incongruous in such a beautiful setting.

Yet whenever he walks by the gravel pit and hears all the commotion, he is struck by the thought that in the storms of life tranquillity can be found.

Saint Francis de Sales said: "Never be in a hurry; do everything quietly and in a calm spirit. Do not lose your inner peace for anything whatsoever, even if your whole world seems upset."

Thursday – ***November 29***

IT'S an odd thing, but have you noticed how often failure can lead to a totally different kind of success? For example, when in 1993 Greg Mortenson was descending from an unsuccessful attempt to reach the summit of K2, he became lost. His life was saved by the inhabitants of a remote, impoverished, East Pakistani village.

Mortenson vowed to repay their help by returning one day to build them a school. It was a promise he was to keep – and it led to other things. Today he is the founder of the charity Pennies For Peace, which works to bring education and real hope for a better future to many poverty-stricken villages.

And if you place that achievement alongside the world's second highest mountain – well, I think that makes the mountain look pretty small!

Friday – ***November 30***

ONE thing I've always particularly liked about our friend Laura is her ability to see the best in everyone. Knowing how difficult that can sometimes be, I once asked her how she managed it.

"My family moved around a lot when I was growing up," she told me, "and I often found it really hard to make friends. Then one day my mother told me about the little prayer of a French Jesuit priest called Pierre Teilhard de Chardin.

"Grant me to recognise in others, Lord God, the radiance of your own face". It never fails to remind me that whatever our differences, we are all children of God. It's simply a matter of looking for the family resemblance."

And if we could all take that attitude, how quickly suspicion and divisions would fade away.

December

Saturday – **December 1**

WHEN Rudyard Kipling was touring the United States, a mocking journalist announced that the author and poet must have earned 100 dollars for every word he'd ever written. He waved a 100 dollar bill at Kipling and defied him to come up with one word that was worth so much. Kipling took the money and said, "Thanks!"

If you don't think "Thanks" is a valuable word, try living without it – then remember how good a real, heartfelt thank you can make you feel.

Sunday – **December 2**

YOUNG Chloe was looking rather thoughtful when she arrived home from Sunday School. "Mum, don't you think that sometimes it can be very difficult to be a good person?" she asked.

Fortunately her mother knew just the right words to say, for as Lawrence G. Lovasik helpfully advises us, achieving "goodness" is a goal that can be attained one step at a time:

"Try to make at least one person happy every day. If you cannot do a kind deed, speak a kind word. If you cannot speak a kind word, think a kind thought. Count up, if you can, the treasure of happiness that you would dispense in a week, in a year, in a lifetime!"

A treasure of purest gold.

Frozen Moment

Monday – **December 3**

HAVE you heard the story of the Canadian farmer who grew award-winning corn? Every year he entered his corn in the state fair and won a blue ribbon.

When asked by an official what his secret was, he explained that he shared his seed corn with his neighbours. The official then wondered why the farmer would share his best seed corn with the people he was competing against each year.

"Well," said the farmer, "the wind picks up pollen from the ripening corn and spreads it from field to field. If my neighbours grow inferior corn, cross-pollination will surely degrade the quality of my corn. If I am to grow a good crop, I know I must, in turn, help my neighbours to grow a good one, too."

We are all connected. If we want to live well, we must help others to live well, for the welfare of each of us is bound up with the welfare of all.

Tuesday – **December 4**

IT might be a word of encouragement at a critical time. It might be to offer shelter or forgiveness. It might be a smile, or it might be some great work. It's possible you might puzzle over the mystery of why you were placed on this earth. But, rest assured, the fact that you are here is important.

A New England novelist wrote these thoughtful words: "Everyone has a unique role to fill in the world and is important in some respect. Everyone, including and perhaps especially you, is indispensable."

The next time you feel down or undervalued, remember, whatever your role in this life might be, you are "indispensable".

Wednesday – **December 5**

OUR old friend Mary cherishes this traditional prayer which she keeps in a well-thumbed scrapbook:

Lord Jesus, I give you my hands to do your work,
I give you my feet to go your way.
I give you my tongue to speak your words.
I give you my mind that you may think in me.
I give you my spirit that you may pray in me.
Above all I give you my heart that you may love in me your Father, and all mankind.
I give you my whole self that you may grow in me, so that
it is you, Lord Jesus, who lives and works and prays in me.

Thursday – **December 6**

IT'S not enough to have lived. We should be determined to live for something. May I suggest that it be creating joy for others, sharing what we have for the betterment of personkind, bringing hope to the lost and love to the lonely.

Leo F. Buscaglia

Friday – **December 7**

MANY people spend so much time trying to live up to other people's expectations and the end result is often a lot of unhappy people. But it doesn't have to be that way.

As a well-known sportsman once said: "One of the things my parents taught me, is never to listen to other people's expectations. You should live your own life and live up to your own expectations."

In other words, be you, and be the best you possibly can be!

Stunning Scarlet

Saturday – **December 8**

"AT the time, it did seem so unfair!" Emily recalled. "There I was, on the verge of leaving for university and then, in just one moment, everything went wrong."

She was speaking of the accident from which it had taken her months to recover, and as a result she had to postpone her studies for a year.

"Well, I was very upset at first," she admitted, "especially when I thought of all my friends studying and also having a good time while I had to wait. But then I came across this quotation that really made me think again: 'You can dance anywhere, even if only in your heart'. I still don't know where it came from, but it seemed as if it had been written just for me."

And that's a lesson we can all take to heart, whatever our circumstances.

Sunday – **December 9**

IT perhaps happens less frequently these days, but every once in a while we get a heavy fall of snow and everything seems to stop. It can be a nuisance but if you are prepared it can also be a restful time. You're not going anywhere – but neither is anybody else!

When the hectic pace of life gets shut down our thoughts often turn to higher things, such as how beautiful the snow is, how good it feels to be alive, how much we love and how much we are loved. On these days when we can't go forwards and we can't go backwards, we might just find ourselves sending quiet thoughts of gratitude upwards.

"Be still, and know that I am God; I will be exalted among the nations, I will be exalted in the earth."

(Psalms 46:10)

Monday – **December 10**

IT'S a beautiful world, and we all have our favourite corners of it. Like many of us, Ron loves visiting the coast and always returns refreshed.

"I don't know which I like best," he smiled. "The sound of the waves, the gulls wheeling in the sky, or just the way those wide horizons seem to put life in proportion.

Jacques Cousteau observed: "The sea, once it casts its spell, holds one in its net of wonder forever."

Whether your preference is for the wonders below the water, or enjoying it from above – or maybe for somewhere altogether drier, make sure you enjoy your favourite part of the world!

Tuesday – **December 11**

HERE are some wise words spoken by Jimmy Carter, the 39th President of the United States from 1977–1981.

"I have one life and one chance to make it count for something. I'm free to choose what that something is, and the something I've chosen is my faith. My faith demands – this is not optional – that I do whatever I can, wherever I am, whenever I can, for as long as I can with whatever I have to try to make a difference."

Wednesday – **December 12**

IT'S an oft-repeated refrain at this time of year. Full of the spirit of the season people ask, "Why can't every day be like Christmas?"

Well, it can! In the words of Dale Evans Rogers: "Christmas, my child, is love in action. Every time we love, every time we give – it's Christmas!"

Thursday — **December 13**

CANDLES have always symbolised remembrance, the dispersal of darkness, goodwill and welcome. On Christmas Eve, the Night of the Candles in a Celtic Scotland, lit candles were placed in windows to guide the Holy Family to the stable in Bethlehem.

Candles were lit again when darkness fell on 31st December, the last day of the Old Year, to show the way and welcome visitors. This idea was echoed in the Celtic benediction: "A fire to warm you by, and a light to guide you."

Words which continue to bring a glow to the heart today.

Friday — **December 14**

IT would surely be a pity if the spirit of giving was only confined to expensive gifts during the festive season. John Greenleaf Whittier sums up that feeling so well:

Somehow not only for Christmas
But all the long year through
The joy that you give to others
Is the joy that comes back to you
And the more you spend in blessing
The poor and lonely and sad
The more of your heart's possessing
Returns to make you glad.

Saturday — **December 15**

WHY is the word "Noel" associated with Christmas? Well, it comes from the French words "les Bonnes Nouvelles", "the Good News".

It's worth remembering that, no matter how commercial it might sometimes seem to us today, The First Noel was the best news the world ever had and Christmas has been Good News ever since!

Sunday – ***December 16***

AT this time of year it's not uncommon to overhear the Lady of the House humming seasonal songs to herself – "Have Yourself A Merry Little Christmas" is a favourite.

"I love the words," she explained. "It doesn't raise unrealistic expectations of the festivities, but it reminds us one of the best ways to celebrate is when 'Faithful friends who are dear to us, gather near to us once more'. And, even if we can't actually 'gather near' in person, we can still use cards and letters to bring us together."

Monday – ***December 17***

O HOLY Night is a much loved Christmas carol and I wonder if you know the story behind its composition?

It was Placide Cappeau, a wine merchant and poet born in 1808 in France, who wrote its words which he called "Minuit, Chrétiens". Placide said he wrote the words on a stagecoach journey to Paris in 1847, which must have been extremely difficult as he had only one hand as the result of a childhood accident.

It was a fellow countryman, the composer of operas and ballets Adolphe Charles Adam, the creator of the ballet "Giselle", who set the words to music and it was first sung at midnight mass on Christmas Eve, 1847, in Roquemaure near Avignon.

In the late 19th century "Minuit, Chrétiens" was translated into English by the American Unitarian clergyman and music critic John S. Dwight and it became known as "O Holy Night". When this carol was broadcast on Christmas Eve in 1906, it was said that it was the first music ever broadcast on radio.

Tuesday — **December 18**

THE Chinese writer, Lin Yutang, was not only an author, but a translator and inventor as well – indeed, he was the first person to create a Chinese typewriter.

So he was certainly hard working and yet he still found time to pen this interesting thought: *Besides the noble art of getting things done, there is the noble art of leaving things undone. The wisdom of life consists in the elimination of non-essentials.*

Wednesday — **December 19**

IF we can ignore time's
fevered progress
and parting the grass find
the meanest flower,
then we might see with
a clearer eye truly
what fulfilment is
simply by facing south and
smiling at all days with
a child's mouth.

John Ellis.

Thursday — **December 20**

CHARLES Dickens' readers loved "A Christmas Carol" in his lifetime as readers still do today, and his other seasonal stories were greatly enjoyed, too. It is from "The Christmas Tree" that I have chosen these words for you.

Christmas is celebrated, his readers are told, "in commemoration of the law of love and kindness, mercy and compassion. This is in remembrance of Me!"

This, I believe, captures the essential spirit of our great festival which celebrates the birth of Christ.

Friday – **December 21**

A CLASS of schoolchildren was asked to write down what they thought were today's Seven Wonders of the World.

While gathering the votes, their teacher noted that one pupil had not finished her exercise, so she asked her if she was finding the task hard. The girl replied, "Yes, a little. I couldn't quite make up my mind because there are so many."

She hesitated, then said: "I think the Seven Wonders of the World are: 'To see', 'To hear', 'To touch', 'To taste', 'To feel', 'To laugh', 'To love'."

A gentle reminder to us all that the most precious things in life cannot be built by hand or bought by man.

Saturday – **December 22**

THE greatest treasures are those invisible to the eye but found by the heart.

Anon

Sunday – **December 23**

CHRISTMAS trees have become inextricably linked with the birth of Jesus across the world. It's an attractive celebration of a joyous occasion – but it isn't the whole story.

To get the full meaning our friend Alex recommends waiting until your (living) tree is ready for recycling, then take off the branches, cut off the top third and tie it across the trunk, forming a cross.

Then, remembering what that innocent baby was born for, say thank you. "The angel said to the women, 'Do not be afraid, for I know that you are looking for Jesus, who was crucified'."

(Matthew 28:5)

Monday – **December 24**

A YOUNG woman is pregnant. She has no proper place to have her baby. A lean-to shed is her only shelter which she shares with some goats and chickens. So there without clean water, on filthy straw, perhaps in bitter cold or raging heat, she gives birth. It's painful, it's lonely, and she's frightened.

Bethlehem? In our nativity cards and dramas and cribs we see what we want to see – clean straw, clean animals, a serene Mary dressed in spotless blue with Joseph looking on, mature and wise.

If it isn't like that in the poorest parts of the world today, then surely it can't have been like that in Bethlehem? Something for us all to think about.

Tuesday – **December 25**

CHRISTMAS is the candle-glow
That lights the darkest gloom,
Christmas is the fireside
That warms the coldest room,
Christmas is the silver star
That guides all those who roam,
Christmas is the shining path
That beckons us back home.
Christmas is the peal of bells,
That spills through frosty air,
Christmas is the greetings card
That shows old friends still care,
Christmas is the fragrant dish
Of joy and hope combined,
Christmas is the gift of love
That's meant for all mankind.

Margaret Ingall

Wednesday – ***December 26***

THE 26th of December is known as Boxing Day, and is also celebrated as St Stephen's Day.

Stephen, a man much loved by those to whom he preached, was seen as a dangerous enemy. He was brought to trial, and later condemned to be stoned to death. Saul of Tarsus watched without pity as Stephen met his fate.

Stephen's death and faith, however, had one unexpected result; later Saul, a Roman citizen, was converted through a life-changing vision on the road to Damascus, and he later became St Paul the Apostle, the renowned missionary and theologian.

For centuries St Stephen has been celebrated as the first Christian martyr, a man who asked that those who stoned him should be forgiven.

Thursday – ***December 27***

THE Lady of the House has been reading a fascinating book by Nick Thorpe who, together with seven crew mates, was inspired by the example of Thor Heyerdahl to sail from South America to Easter Island in a boat made of reeds. It was a risky venture, and Nick's decision to participate was not taken lightly.

When discussing the proposition with his wife and facing its uncertainties, he says that they both "remembered what they did believe: that God wouldn't necessarily intervene to stop you drowning, but he'd be there alongside you, whether in this life or the next. God was love, and love was stronger than fear."

An inspiring thought, and for readers who do like to be sure of the outcome, Nick and all the crew of the *Viracocha* did enjoy – and survive – their adventure!

Northern Lights

Friday – **December 28**

IT had been a difficult time for our friend Adrian. Illness and redundancy had cast a shadow over his life, and his self-confidence had taken a knock. But gradually, he began to look just that little bit more self-assured.

"It was when I was at my lowest that a friend advised me to go for a walk round the park each day," he told me. "At first I found it a real chore, but gradually I discovered that I wasn't just looking forward to it, I was also feeling much better about everything. Isn't it amazing how nature puts everything into perspective?"

Environmentalist Rachel Carson once said: "Those who contemplate the beauty of the earth find reserves of strength that will endure as long as life lasts."

Saturday – **December 29**

A CLERGYMAN of a large, centuries'-old church was showing a class of children from a nearby primary school around, pointing out many things of interest.

One young lad, clearly overwhelmed by the sheer scale of the massive building, called out, "It's so big! Is this your church?"

"No, it's yours," came the reply.

Later he wondered how many of his congregation realised this, so he put up a notice on the front door: *Welcome to your Church.*

It attracted a lot of attention, so he put up another notice a few weeks later:

What are you seeking? Is it love, understanding, friendship, acceptance, belonging, kindness or forgiveness? Whatever it is, congratulations, you've found it. Come on in!

Something for us all to think about today.

Sunday – **December 30**

MIKE told me about being out in his car and getting caught in a snowstorm. Halfway to his destination, just when he was about to give up, pull over and wait until the storm had passed, a snowplough took to the road ahead of him.

Reassured by the very sight of the heavy machinery, Mike decided to follow it as far as he could. The falling snow was so thick that at times he couldn't even see the snowplough's flashing lights clearly, but the road stayed clear – all the way home!

There are times in life when our troubles can seem to surround us, perhaps even stop us in our tracks, but we have Someone mightier than a snowplough clearing the way for us. And if we follow, both when we see Him and when we can't, He will take us all the way home!

"Then spake Jesus again to them, saying, I am the light of the world: he that followeth me shall not walk in darkness, but shall have the light of life." (John 8:12)

Monday – **December 31**

THE twilight days of December are a good time to remember friends who are no longer with us as we celebrate the arrival of a new year. As the clock strikes midnight each year, our friend John gently halts the merriment to propose this thoughtful toast:

"Let's remember our lost loved ones; let us call up the good memories of happy times spent with now absent family and friends.

"And let us remember how we can still see and hear their faces, remember their jokes, and feel the warmth of their love."

Photograph Locations and Photographers

SNOW AND SILHOUETTE – *Crichton Gardens, Dumfries.*

SCOTTISH SPLENDOUR – *Glen Coe, looking across to the Three Sisters.*

GOLDEN FRINGE – *By the River Severn.*

NEARLY THERE – *Arisaig, Inverness-shire.*

LIGHT IN THE DARKNESS – *St Magnus' Cathedral, Orkney.*

TRANQUILLITY – *Loch Etive and Glen Etive.*

REST AWHILE – *Applecross, Wester Ross.*

CROSSING THE THRESHOLD – *Caerlaverock Castle, Dumfriesshire.*

PERFECT PEACE – *St Ronan's Bay, Iona.*

SET IN STONE – *The Cathedral of St Michael and St Gudula, Brussels.*

SHARE THIS MOMENT – *View from Salter's Hill, Gloucestershire over the Vale of Evesham.*

HOMECOMING – *Fortingall, Perthshire.*

TIME FOR REFLECTION – *Culloden House, Inverness.*

GREEN AND GOLD – *Stock Ghyll, Ambleside.*

MORLICH MAGNIFICENCE – *The Cairngorms from Loch Morlich.*

NORTHERN LIGHTS – *Aberdeen.*

ACKNOWLDEGEMENTS: **David Askham;** Smooth As Silk, Parade Of Pink, A Corner In Crete, From The Orchard, Stunning Scarlet. **V. K. Guy;** Let's Go For A Walk! **C. R. Kilvington;** Share This Moment. **Douglas Laidlaw;** Festival Finery, Nearly There, Shelter From The Storm, Crossing The Threshold, Perfect Peace. **Frédéric Lion;** Set In Stone. **Duncan I. McEwan;** Light In The Darkness, Rest Awhile, Homecoming, The Turning, Frozen Moment. **Polly Pullar;** Her Little Lambs. **SW Images;** Snow And Silhouette, Scottish Splendour, Sweet Nectar. **Sheila Taylor;** Northern Lights. **Jack Watson;** Tranquillity, Time For Reflection, Morlich Magnificence. **Richard Watson;** Seeking The Sunlight, Golden Fringe, Take Care!, Green And Gold.

Published by D.C. Thomson Annuals Ltd., in 2011
D.C. Thomson Annuals Ltd.,
Courier Buildings
2 Albert Square
Dundee DD1 9QJ
Printed in China